Your Guide to Eliminating Negative Thinking

The Proven Techniques to Overcome Negativity, Reshaping Your Mind, Changing Your Thoughts, Mastering the Art of Self-Affirmation, and Cultivating Positivity

Larin Carney

© **Copyright 2023 - All rights reserved.**

The content contained within this book may not be reproduced, duplicated or transmitted without direct written permission from the author or the publisher.

Under no circumstances will any blame or legal responsibility be held against the publisher, or author, for any damages, reparation, or monetary loss due to the information contained within this book, either directly or indirectly.

Legal Notice:

This book is copyright protected. It is only for personal use. You cannot amend, distribute, sell, use, quote or paraphrase any part, or the content within this book, without the consent of the author or publisher.

Disclaimer Notice:

Please note the information contained within this document is for educational and entertainment purposes only. All effort has been executed to present accurate, up to date, reliable, complete information. No warranties of any kind are declared or implied. Readers acknowledge that the author is not engaged in the rendering of legal, financial, medical or professional advice. The content within this book has been derived from various sources. Please consult a licensed professional before attempting any techniques outlined in this book.

By reading this document, the reader agrees that under no circumstances is the author responsible for any losses, direct or indirect, that are incurred as a result of the use of the information contained within this document, including, but not limited to, errors, omissions, or inaccuracies.

Table of Contents

INTRODUCTION 1
    YOUR PHYSICAL ENVIRONMENT IS JUST AS REAL AS YOUR MENTAL ONE 2
    YOU'RE RESPONSIBLE FOR WHAT LIVES IN YOUR MIND RENT-FREE 3
    YOU'RE NOT ALONE 3
    A SOLUTION TO YOUR PROBLEMS 4

CHAPTER 1: UNDERSTANDING NEGATIVE THOUGHTS 7
    WHAT CAUSES NEGATIVE THOUGHT PATTERNS? 8
        Four Main Factors That Cause Negative Thought Patterns 9
    MENTAL HEALTH DISORDERS THAT INTENSIFY NEGATIVE THINKING 16
        Obsessive Compulsive Disorder (OCD) 16
        Generalized Anxiety Disorder (GAD) 18
        Depression 21
    EXAMPLES OF NEGATIVE THINKING PATTERNS 23
        What the Fruit Now Looks Like 23
    HABITS THAT LEAD TO COGNITIVE DISTORTION 30
        Overthinking 31
        Rumination 32
        Cyclical Hostility 33
    BREAKING NEGATIVE THINKING PATTERNS 33
        Scheduling Negative Thinking 34
        Replace Bad Thoughts 35
        Love Yourself 36
        Journaling 36
        Be Honest With Yourself 37
        Exercise and Meditation 37
    CHAPTER SUMMARY 38

CHAPTER 2: FACING THE ENEMY WITHIN BY IDENTIFYING YOUR NEGATIVE THOUGHTS 39
    JUMPING TO CONCLUSIONS 40
    CATASTROPHIZING 41
    OVERGENERALIZATION 43
    EMOTIONAL REASONING 44
    LABELING 45
    CHAPTER SUMMARY 47

CHAPTER 3: RESHAPING YOUR MIND BY REPLACING THE NEGATIVE THOUGHTS 49

INTRODUCING BLUE AND TRUE THOUGHTS 50
- BLUE Thoughts 50
- TRUE Thoughts 52

PRACTICAL WAYS TO RESHAPE YOUR NEGATIVE THOUGHTS 53
- The Two-Column Technique 53
- New Evidence 54
- Self-Compassion 55
- Socratic Questions 55
- Self-Acceptance 56

CHAPTER SUMMARY 56

CHAPTER 4: BE YOUR OWN BEST FRIEND 59

THE RAIN TECHNIQUE 61

HOW TO BECOME YOUR OWN BEST FRIEND 63
- Get to Know Yourself 63
- Respond to Your Needs 63
- Understand That Being Your Own Best Friend Isn't an Act of Selfishness 64
- Engage in Self-Care 65
- Be Honest With Yourself 66

CHAPTER SUMMARY 66

CHAPTER 5: SWEAT AWAY THE NEGATIVITY BY EXERCISING TO FIGHT NEGATIVE THINKING 69

UNDERSTANDING THOUGHT EXERCISES 70
- Thought Exercises That Will Boost Your Mental Health 71

ADDITIONAL WAYS TO FIGHT NEGATIVE THINKING 76
- Write It Down 76
- Focus On It 76
- Notice the Thought 76
- Question Your Thinking 77
- Think Two for One 77

CHAPTER SUMMARY 78

CHAPTER 6: UNRAVELING THE MIND BY DEFEATING NEGATIVE THINKING WITH COMMUNICATION 79

HOW COMMUNICATION CAN RESHAPE YOUR SELF-TALK 80
- A Communication Breakdown 81

IMPROVING THE COMMUNICATION YOU HAVE WITH YOURSELF 83
- Focus on What You Are Feeling Right Now 83
- Share Your Feelings With Someone Close to You 83
- Treat Yourself 84

> Take Time to Count Your Blessings 84
> Make Social Connections 84
> CHAPTER SUMMARY 85

CHAPTER 7: THE POWER OF COMPASSION WHEN YOU FIND A WAY TO SERVE 87

> THE BENEFITS OF EXERCISING COMPASSION ON OTHERS 88
> Improves Your Physical and Mental Health 88
> Strengthens Relationships 89
> A Just Society 89
> Personal Growth 90
> DIFFERENT WAYS TO SERVE OTHERS 90
> Donations 91
> Feeding the Hungry 92
> Mentor 92
> Volunteer Your Services 93
> Brighten Someone's Day 93
> CHAPTER SUMMARY 94

CHAPTER 8: HARNESSING THE POWER OF GRATITUDE AS A SHIELD AGAINST NEGATIVE THINKING 95

> DIFFERENT WAYS TO CULTIVATE A HABIT OF GRATITUDE 96
> Keep a Gratitude Journal 96
> Remember the Bad 97
> Try to Notice When You Feel Grateful 97
> Consider Reflecting on What You're Grateful for 97
> Smile More Often 98
> CHAPTER SUMMARY 98

CHAPTER 9: WRITE DOWN WHAT YOU'RE FEELING 99

> HOW TO BEGIN AND SUSTAIN YOUR JOURNALING HABIT 101
> Commit to Writing Every Day 101
> Arrange a Time and Possibly a Location for Journaling 101
> Set a Time Limit 102
> Be Flexible 102
> CHAPTER SUMMARY 102

CHAPTER 10: EMBRACING CHANGE BY BUILDING NEW HABITS TO COMBAT NEGATIVE THINKING 105

> WHAT EMBRACING CHANGE CAN DO FOR YOU 105
> Growth in All Aspects of Your Life 105
> Adaptability and Flexibility 106
> Validation and Re-evaluation 106
> Exposing Your Strengths 106
> Lessons and Failures 106

  The Guts to Achieve More *107*
  Handling Setbacks and Appreciating Success *107*
 DIFFERENT WAYS YOU CAN WORK ON EMBRACING CHANGE 107
  Examples of Good Habits *108*
  Write Down Your Goals *108*
  Build Good Habits Into Your Routine *109*
  Reflect on Your Habits *109*
  Develop Self-Discipline *109*
 CHAPTER SUMMARY 110

CHAPTER 11: MASTERING THE ART OF SELF-AFFIRMATION 111

 USING POSITIVE AFFIRMATIONS 112
  How to Use Positive Affirmations *112*
  Set Them in the Present *112*
  Avoid Stock Affirmations *113*
  Keep It Real *113*
  Practice Affirming Yourself Every Day *113*
 CHAPTER SUMMARY 114

CHAPTER 12: MINDFULNESS AND BEYOND—EMPOWERING YOUR MIND WITH MEDITATION 115

 DIFFERENT WAYS TO PRACTICE MINDFULNESS AND MEDITATION 116
  Let Your Body Relax *116*
  Focus on Pleasure and Not Pain *116*
  Gently Observe Your Negative Thoughts *116*
  Breathe Deep *117*
  Meditate at the Same Time Every Day *117*
 CHAPTER SUMMARY 117

CONCLUSION 119

REFERENCES 121

Introduction

I want you to imagine driving home one afternoon after a long day's work. As you approach your driveway, you suddenly notice bits of litter all over your lawn, and while trying to look around to see if any suspicious behavior or person is lurking around, nothing looks out of the ordinary. As you exit your car to make sense of the situation, you can't seem to find answers to any of the questions that you are asking yourself. But amid all the confusion, you'll likely pick up the litter and clean your lawn either way.

Say it's the next day, and you're driving back home again after a long day at work. As you approach your driveway, you notice the same litter cluttering your lawn. And again, there's no unusual behavior or suspect in sight as you look around to find the culprit who has done this. As you prepare yourself to clean up the litter, even more questions begin to cloud your mind. And this time around, you may start thinking of ways to catch the culprit and handle the situation. By now, you may have gone to the extent of asking a few neighbors if they noticed anything out of the ordinary. But with a few ideas and plans in motion, you'll still collect the litter and clean the mess.

Let's say it's now the third day, and again, you approach your driveway and find the same litter all over your lawn, just like the last two days. This time around, you feel yourself boiling on the inside as you try to make sense of the situation. With no option but to collect the litter and clean up the mess for the third time this week, traps, a higher fence, and vicious dogs may cross your mind as you plan to hunt this culprit down until they're found.

Your Physical Environment Is Just as Real as Your Mental One

Looking back at the scenario with the lawn and clutter, I'd like you to identify with all the emotions, thoughts, and efforts that I've expressed. Do you believe you would have felt the same? Do you believe you also would have questioned yourself and thought about who could have done this and why someone would suddenly want to spite you in this way? Do you believe you would also have started devising plans on how to discourage, catch, or punish the culprit?

By answering yes to any of these questions, I'd like you to realize the efforts we make, as human beings, to take care of our physical environments. The moment we find any litter or clutter in our personal spaces, like our homes, cars, and lawns, we make a significant effort to create order, even if it means having to "clean a mess that's been made by someone else." Also, when we find this litter and clutter is a consistent problem, it only takes three days to put plans in place to find the root cause of our problem and deal with it.

But how much effort do we make to clean, organize, and invest in our minds? Now replace your lawn with your mind, the culprit with the individuals and spaces we expose ourselves to, and your neighbors, fences, and dogs with support systems. How much effort do we make to keep our minds healthy, balanced, and positive? How quick are we to get to the bottom of our triggers, negative thoughts, and emotions? And how often do we become proactive in "cleaning up the mess" even when we aren't the ones who made it? Usually, when it comes to our minds, we leave the litter there long enough to poison the lawn if we don't find ourselves personally responsible for "creating the mess." We then blame everything and everyone else for the condition of our minds while making little to no effort to "clean up the mess" ourselves.

You're Responsible for What Lives in Your Mind Rent-Free

Circumstances, trauma, and experiences do a lot to shape who we are today because from then on, we either grow as people or become the worst versions of ourselves. It's important to realize that even though you won't be in control of what goes on in the world and the individuals who inhabit it, you do have full control over your choices, lessons, and actions that you take. This means that even with you not knowing who the culprit is, you're still responsible for ensuring that the spaces and people you surround yourself with don't poison your mind. That's *your* responsibility.

Like the culprits who will never return to admit their wrongs, explain their actions, and make it up to you, the people and spaces that poison our minds with clutter never return to make right of their wrongs. But the big question is, how do you turn out in the long run? What would happen to your lawn if you simply parked your car, threw a little fit outside, and went straight inside without cleaning up the litter? Would it create a foul smell? Yes. Would it look disturbing? Yes? Would it rot? Yes. Would it attract all sorts of bugs and flies? Yes. So, what do you think happens when we don't make the effort to clear our negative thoughts?

You're Not Alone

Like you, many have come a long way in realizing that they're responsible for the change and balance that they're looking for. Like many other people, we grow up with dreams, goals, and aspirations; however, regardless of all the hard and physical work that we put into achieving our dreams, goals, and aspirations, it's self-doubt, confusion, and other negative thoughts and emotions that lead us to points of feeling drained, overwhelmed, and unable to do more.

When we ask ourselves why we feel the way we do, attract the same situations and people, and respond the same way each time, it's then that we tap into understanding what negative thinking is and how it affects our lives in the long run. Sure, some good news, a new hobby, and a better-paying job can spark more positive thinking; however, if you're constantly sinking into negative thinking, it may be because of underlying issues that cannot necessarily be solved with news of a new apartment, choosing to travel more, or receiving more money. These are only temporary solutions to a lifelong problem.

Unfortunately, making a conscious decision to work on your mental state won't be as easy, straightforward, or quick as peeling an onion. Yes, you'll be uncovering yourself layer by layer, but the years that went into influencing your present negative thoughts won't change with just a few therapy sessions or a few days of meditating. Even though many others have walked their journey and sought change long before now, they still find themselves on the journey because we're all still yet to face experiences that may take us back to where we were initially. Therefore, it's important to be intentional, committed, and consistent in every effort that we make to change our negative mindsets, because this will involve a lot of unlearning and relearning.

A Solution to Your Problems

Instead of throwing you a few tips and tricks while encouraging you to meditate because "It's all in the mind" and "It starts with you," my guidelines aim to take you through a journey of transformation. By uncovering all there is to know about having a negative mindset, I've structured everything to accommodate any weaknesses, background, and demographic so that regardless of where you may be mentally, you can always come back to this book and revisit the principles, practices, and ideas that may help you at different points on your quest. So, in addition to helping you understand what negative thoughts are and how they shape the way you behave in your physical environment, we'll also be tackling root causes, how you respond to yourself in situations, how to channel negative experiences, the importance of communication, how compassion is beneficial to you and others, finding power in gratitude, how to embrace change, and more.

Apart from being exceptionally excited about our journey together, I want you to know that I'm deeply passionate about this topic because I know and understand how it changed my life. Therefore, I'm hoping that it will do the same for you in every way possible.

Chapter 1:

Understanding Negative Thoughts

Let's take a moment to think about the scenario with you and your lawn again. We often believe our surroundings are the sole influencers of our thoughts and emotions while neglecting to realize that we also have a part to play in understanding why we think and feel the way we do. So think of it this way: In the event of your lawn appearing unkempt, cluttered, and neglected, are others, like the mysterious culprit, solely responsible for having it become that way? In other words, do lawns only reach a stage of neglect and clutter when someone else comes around to mess it up? Of course not.

When we don't make an effort to maintain our lawn, we also become the reason why it suddenly appears unkempt, cluttered, and neglected. In that light, it's not enough to blame our thoughts and emotions on what we're exposed to and how others treat us. We have a large part to play in influencing that part of our lives. Since we have limited control over what goes on in the world and the decisions people make, taking control of your life goes as far as controlling and having power over what goes on within you.

Positive mindsets, manifestation, and personal transformation are some of the most powerful techniques people adopt to take control of their minds and emotions. However, these techniques don't prove to be effective and sustainable over time if you don't take time to figure out the reason you think and feel the way you do. By making yourself aware of the triggers, trauma, and personal experiences that lead you to develop negative thoughts and emotions regarding certain circumstances, you can eliminate negative thinking through healing and change.

What Causes Negative Thought Patterns?

When we're unable to address, heal, and manage traumatic past experiences, anxieties, and fears, these automatically turn into repetitive, unhelpful thoughts that we know as negative thought patterns. Many of us make the mistake of thinking bad experiences are only "part of life" and exist "to make us stronger." However, if we don't work to heal these negative experiences, they turn into invasive emotions that we later struggle to function with. Over time, these thoughts and emotions contribute to even worse forms of anxiety and fear, since they usually lead people to points of depression, stress, low self-confidence, and unworthiness.

You can be conscious and unconscious of your negative thoughts. With conscious thoughts, this feels something similar to an inside voice that you can hear in your head. So, this would be similar to finding yourself thinking, *I'm not attractive enough* or *I'm never good at anything I do*. On the other hand, your unconscious negative thoughts are silent and usually show up and play out as a response to something. This is because they operate in the background of what we're aware of, which is in the subconscious part of our minds. Typically triggered by a negative experience, old conditioning, and internal belief systems, these unconscious thoughts stay dormant for long periods. However, when you're confronted with a situation that triggers it, you find yourself immediately responding to the situation in a strong and sometimes aggressive manner. Unfortunately, unconscious negative thoughts aren't easy to identify because people usually notice them only after identifying a repeated pattern of emotion and action toward a certain event, person, or situation. It's usually only when things escalate to the point of being damaging that people desire to find the underlying situation of their thoughts and emotions.

Positive and negative internal thought patterns are often conversational, situational, and able to influence the way we view, understand, and experience different relationships and environments. So, think of it this way: Seed qualities vary due to seed vigor, which determines the overall quality and performance of the seed as it's germinating and emerging. This means that not all seeds will produce high-quality fruit. With high-vigor seeds, which represent positive mindsets, thoughts, and emotions, these will germinate into good fruit. However, low-vigor seeds, which represent negative mindsets, thoughts, and emotions, will germinate into bad fruit. In that light, it's unhealthy for us to limit our view of the impact of negative thought patterns to throwing a little temper tantrum, having a bad day, or not "feeling like yourself." These thought patterns are a lot more damaging than we think. The size of a fruit is always larger than that of its seed; therefore, ignoring or entertaining negative thinking patterns only grows into something larger over time, and with low-vigor seeds, this will germinate into a large bad fruit.

Four Main Factors That Cause Negative Thought Patterns

Before we can look at the effects that negative thought patterns have on us, we have to start by understanding what causes them. No one is born with negative ideas about how they feel about themselves and those around them. These are fueled by experiences, people, and experiences that we categorize into four main factors.

Anxiety and Worry

We become anxious when we worry about uncertainties that we have no control over. When this happens, we often spend our time obsessing or entertaining negative ideas that only worsen what we're thinking and how we're feeling. Unfortunately, like depression, most people lack the emotional support they need while struggling with anxiety, and this leads them to either seek professional help, find distractions to help them cope with the condition, or, like most people, try to stop the thoughts by not giving them any attention. Of course, working with a professional can be helpful in the long run; however, remember that stopping or ignoring your anxiety may work for now but over time, it could worsen your negative thinking.

Having negative thoughts from time to time is natural to all of us, but these bad ideas become a problem when they start to affect how you see and treat yourself and those around you. When you find yourself entertaining the same negative thought over and over again, this should be a sign that there may be some underlying issues that urgently need your attention.

According to research, repetitive negative thoughts come in two forms: worry and rumination *(Anxiety and Negative Thoughts, n.d.)*. When you worry, you have recurring thoughts that leave you feeling uneasy and nervous. It's here that your mind begins to flood itself with negative ideas suggesting that a bad experience is on the way. In other words, worry concerns itself about the future. On the other hand, there is rumination, which is slightly different from worry in the sense that it's the feeling of worry that concerns itself with the past. Here, you find yourself feeling uneasy and nervous about events that have already happened. This means pondering over thoughts that remind you of how poorly you did something or how guilty you feel for treating someone in a certain way.

Worry and rumination are relatively different from one another; however, the one thing they have in common is that they encourage the mind to form repetitive ideas about ourselves, loved ones, finances, or careers that aren't helpful or of use to us in any way. It's possible for someone to have worry and rumination within them at the same time because both these forms of anxiety involve uncontrollable, intrusive, prolonged, and repetitive thoughts that all concern themselves about what's already happened and what's going to happen.

Anxiety can have you feeling flooded with a whole lot of worry without anything actually happening. It's in your imagination that you'll find yourself thinking about what you need to do just to prevent the worst from happening; sometimes, you go looking for reasons to feel a sense of panic and stress when nothing seems to be occupying your mind at the time. Anxiety and stress disorders can have you feeling a sense of dread and doom while suffering from physical symptoms, including trembling, heart palpitations, sleep disorders, and hyperventilation. Fortunately, support and treatment can help individuals overcome these negative thoughts in the long run.

Ruminating

Ruminating is when we think deeply about something. So, when you introduce this in the context of what this means with negative thought patterns, it simply means you are making a habit of pondering over mistakes, problems, and misfortunes that have happened in the past. By not moving on from these events, the thoughts and emotions of it all have you feeling like you have a growing monkey sitting on your shoulder.

Part of maintaining a healthy way of living means reflecting on situations now and then to see what you could have done differently to do better in future instances. However, rumination is far from this because while you're reflecting on your poor choices, inappropriate behavior, or embarrassing moments, you can't seem to move past them. You won't find yourself searching for reasons to explain why things turned out the way they did or solutions to prevent you from making that mistake again. Instead, all you do is allow these moments to play out in your mind over and over again while you sit in complete regret and shame over what happened. While you may think your pondering over the situation will go away after a few weeks of thinking about it, those who ruminate over mistakes can do this even five years after the event has taken place!

We will struggle to accept our current realities and find the strength and confidence to move on with our lives if we're trapped in a never-ending thought loop of regret. And unfortunately, the moon and sun don't suddenly pause to allow you the opportunity to trap yourself physically just as you have mentally. Life moves on. However, with you mentally trapped in this loop of regret, this affects how you think and feel about yourself. This is when you'll start to feel a large sense of guilt, shame, and worthlessness over situations you're unable to change.

Those who wish to learn and grow as individuals will reflect on their past experiences in a constructive, mature, and healthy way. But the effort becomes unhealthy and meaningless when you choose to dwell over experiences repeatedly with no plans to learn or grow from them. That's because all you're doing is punishing yourself for something you cannot change, and when this goes on long enough, it brings you inner pain and hinders your ability to move on and be the best version of yourself.

Self-Criticism and Feelings of Worthlessness

A voice exists in every one of us, and depending on the condition of our minds, this voice can either be empowering or destructive. With thoughts running through our minds day in and day out, this voice can help guide us into solving problems and achieving our goals. But it's when we aren't careful and intentional about the condition of our minds that the voice inside us turns into our worst enemy. When this happens, it turns into our worst critic and often bullies us into feeling low, undeserving, and not enough. It also creates self-doubt by always pointing out our flaws and having us question everything that we do in our lives.

To understand the harsh and brutal depth of our negative voices, I'd like you to think of a negative comment your inner voice often tells you. Now, I'd like you to ask yourself, "Would I say this to the next person?" Chances are you wouldn't dare to speak like that to someone else because you know what impact that would have on them. So, take a moment to look into what these harsh and brutal comments do to you on the inside. Knowing that we often make mistakes and experience regular setbacks, think about the number of times a day you're being bullied and harassed by your inner voice. This not only magnifies any flaws and weaknesses that you have but it also adds an element of suffering to a situation you already wish you could change.

When you entertain self-criticism and negative self-talk long enough, this affects how you feel about yourself. With positive self-talk, you feel good about yourself and work to invest in all spheres of your life while rewarding yourself for the efforts you make. Once you entertain negative self-talk, how you treat yourself changes. Because your mind is clouded with judgment, shame, and regret, you're unable to do anything meaningful for yourself, and this will keep you from making any effort to invest in yourself, whether it's physically, emotionally, mentally, spiritually, or financially. Over time, this lack of self-care will remove the need for you to reward yourself for anything you do because you'll always feel undeserving and unworthy of anything good and positive in your life. Therefore, by depriving yourself of reward for all you do, you turn into your own slave, and that automatically attacks your self-esteem and self-confidence without you realizing it. When we reach points of feeling completely hopeless about there being any chance of rescue from this trap that we feel stuck in, this leads us to depression and sometimes suicide, as we no longer see any reason for living.

Many people make the mistake of believing that self-criticism is self-improvement, but this is far from true. When we think of self-criticism, we immediately confuse it with constructive criticism, but let's take a moment to understand the two. Criticism on its own is damaging because it means people are expressing their disapproval by highlighting any faults and mistakes that they've found with someone or something. But its effect can be empowering when it's turned into constructive criticism, where a person can express their disapproval by highlighting any faults and mistakes that they find while also offering added feedback that will allow for improvement; however, it's important to note that constructive criticism doesn't mean sugar-coating or withholding any truth. The opinion one expresses should remain blunt and honest, and they should be sure they're offering feedback that will create room for improvement.

When we talk about self-criticism, there isn't anything constructive about it because you're shaming and judging yourself repeatedly with no intention of thinking of a solution to your problem. So, when we talk about self-criticism, this is nowhere near constructive criticism. By taking a moment to understand what self-improvement is, you learn that it's a conscious effort you make to develop and improve your knowledge, character, and status. All this requires you to have a positive mindset that will thrive off of positive thoughts and emotions that you have about yourself. Since self-criticism already stems from negative thought patterns and a negative mindset, we know that self-criticism and self-improvement do not necessarily work to achieve the same goal.

With self-improvement, everything is centered around doing your best while operating within your limits and means. But with self-criticism, because your headspace is filled with ideas about you not doing or being enough, you don't respect or honor your limits and boundaries because you want to feel worthy and enough. So, when we achieve our goals, gain more knowledge, better our status, and build our character, we don't reward ourselves the same as we would if we were operating in a different and more positive headspace. When you decide that these improvements will fill the void you have within yourself, you find yourself constantly wanting to do more because you think doing more will finally get you to the point where you no longer feel empty, worthless, and not enough. But by not addressing the actual cause of the problem, it just becomes a never-ending cycle of you pushing your limits, achieving more, and desiring more in the end. Unfortunately, if you don't take time to realize what you're doing to yourself, you may push yourself to the point of a complete breakdown.

Feeling worthy and deserving of positive outcomes and experiences isn't attained by achieving more. When we rely on our accomplishments to build our self-esteem and confidence, our self-worth grows short when we have setbacks and disappointments across various aspects of our lives. True self-worth is understanding and knowing your willing spirit to thrive in any situation and circumstance, regardless of whether the outcome is positive or negative. This will help you live life in a meaningful, authentic, and whole way.

Obsessing Over Problems and Focusing on the Negative

We usually develop negative thoughts about experiences that aren't going too well in our lives, and when we feel like there's no real solution to our problems, we glue ourselves to them. In the event of this happening, our problems appear more difficult, unpleasant and magnified, and when we achieve small milestones, we don't regard them because we've placed greater priority and focus on our problems and everything else that's going wrong in our lives.

To move away from obsessing over your problems and focusing on the negative, it's important to shift your focus toward everything worth being grateful for. When we have large problems, we often desire solutions or milestones that are just as significant to shift our focus, and only then do we focus on the positive. So, someone with a financial problem will only rejoice when they finally get that higher-paying job, or someone who just got out of a tough breakup will only "feel alive again" when they find another relationship. Instead of acknowledging and appreciating the fact that you have shelter and food for the month or focusing on the lesson that you learned from breaking free from that abusive relationship, you refuse to shift your focus onto more positive things because you require your shift to only take place when it's just as great as the problem.

So, here's a quick story. A teacher once walked into her classroom full of students. After everyone settled down, she took a glass of water and held it in her hand. As she did that, she asked her students, "After two minutes of holding this glass, do you believe this glass of water is heavy for me?" Her students responded by saying, "No." She then asked them if they thought the glass would feel heavy after an hour of holding it, and they said "No." She then asked them if the glass would feel heavy after 24 hours of holding it, and many were unsure of how to respond to the question, but some of them started answering, "Yes." After asking all the questions, the teacher put the glass down and went on to explain that like the glass of water, our problems aren't heavy to us when we hold onto them for just a few minutes. You may start to feel different after an hour of holding onto them, but by the time a day goes by with you holding onto your problems and negative thoughts, they feel heavy and may even bring you to the point of feeling numb.

In that light, it's important to know that obsessing over your problems or focusing on the negative long enough will only leave you feeling numb and paralyzed. It won't fix the problem in any way, shape, or form. Instead, it robs you of an opportunity to make the best of your present moment and refuses you the chance to appreciate everything worth being grateful for. It's impossible to have your mind focusing on both positive and negative thought patterns at the same time. It's either one or the other. And like the situation with the seed and the fruit, what you choose to entertain grows in your mind and starts to bear fruits when you focus on it. Don't let yourself think that a little negative thought you're focusing on will remain just that—small. It will grow and show itself to you in emotion, thought, and action.

Mental Health Disorders That Intensify Negative Thinking

When negative thought patterns become a regular and uncontrollable habit, they intensify and lead many people to points of suffering from a range of mental illnesses, such as anxiety disorders, schizophrenia, personality disorders, and depression. Unfortunately, mental health disorders don't just show up as a product of not addressing negative thought patterns. If you already suffer from mental health disorders, this can intensify and worsen your negative thought patterns. Therefore, in addition to having past traumatic experiences, anxiety about the present, or fears about the future, mental health disorders can magnify all the critical thoughts that you may be having about yourself.

Obsessive Compulsive Disorder (OCD)

OCD is the irresistible urge people have to perform a certain act or task *(What Causes Negative Thinking and How to Stop It, n.d.)*. Usually, it is thought that these tasks work to prevent some kind of mishap or harm from happening, and they're often ineffective and somewhat unnecessary. This urge will arise each time they experience a repeated pattern of entertaining unwanted and intrusive thoughts. Here, the mental health disorder comes in three main elements, which are

- obsessions over any distressing, intrusive, and unwanted thoughts, urges, or images that enter one's mind repeatedly.

- emotions that cause one to feel insanely distressed or anxious.

- compulsions that cause repetitive acts physically and mentally.

All in all, OCD attacks exist to help an individual relieve any kind of anxiety that they may have; however, this relief is very short-lived because the anxiety and obsession return shortly after, and that's how the disorder becomes a cycle.

When it comes to OCD, people will usually experience the compulsions and obsessive ideas that come with it, but most times, one element will appear far more obvious than the other.

Compulsive Behavior

A compulsion will begin when an individual finds ways to prevent or reduce their anxiety through performing acts that are unrealistically connected or excessive. Because they use these behaviors to address any obsessive thoughts that they may have, the urge to perform the act intensifies because they either want to stop the anxiety or prevent it "just in case it returns." So, people who fear germs, contamination, and infection may find themselves washing their hands several times an hour because they just want to neutralize the thought of something happening to them. As an outsider who washes their hands only when it's necessary, this kind of behavior will come off as irrational and illogical. Also, not all compulsions will appear obvious to others.

Many of us have limited perceptions of OCD that is characterized by compulsive urges people have to clean or organize things; however, the mental health disorder does manifest differently in many ways, some of which include the following:

- double-checking
- counting
- hand washing
- arranging
- requiring reassurance
- hoarding
- repeating specific words in your head
- entertaining thoughts you believe will help counter ideas you obsess over

- avoiding situations and places that you believe trigger your obsessive thoughts

Obsessive Thoughts

Aside from the usual negative thoughts and feelings, we also have moments of obsessing over unpleasant or unwanted ideas, like when we come across a violent or offensive image that has us thinking about it for some time, or when we forget to lock the door before leaving the house and find ourselves thinking of the worst the entire day. Behaviors like these are normal. However, obsessive thinking becomes dangerous when it dominates our thinking to the extent that we're incapable of thinking of other things. Common obsessions that have been identified in people with OCD include

- a fear of harming yourself or those around you on purpose.

- a fear of placing yourself or those around you in danger accidentally.

- a fear of getting an infection from a disease or harmful substance.

- the need to keep everything in an orderly or symmetrical fashion.

- a fear of being violated physically or sexually.

Unless these are repetitive thoughts stemming from a previous bad experience, these thoughts remain just that—thoughts. And just because they live in your mind rent-free doesn't mean they will happen. Obsessive thoughts remain unhealthy as they cause one a lot of distress that ultimately affects their quality of life.

Generalized Anxiety Disorder (GAD)

GAD is another mental health disorder that magnifies negative thinking patterns. Here, a person will experience an unsettling sense of anxiety and worry regarding every aspect of their life. So, whether they're going through a rough patch or seemingly doing well, they will make a habit of entertaining fearful mental habits relating to the future. Like OCD, your critical thoughts do become less controllable over time, and once they reach the point of being difficult to control, they start to affect your overall quality of life.

Like most mental health issues, anyone can develop GAD at any stage of their life, whether it's a child or an adult. Here, symptoms can be similar to those found with panic disorders, different types of anxieties, and OCD. However, this doesn't make any of these conditions the same. So, with GAD, you can expect mental symptoms to include

- persistent worry about parts of your life that aren't justified by the impact certain events would have on you.

- devising plans and solutions to any worst-case scenario that you can think of.

- believing most events and situations pose a threat to your life even when they don't.

- finding it hard to handle situations you're unsure of.

- being undecided and fearful of making the wrong choices.

- finding it hard to let go of fear and worry.

- being unable to relax because you're constantly restless and feeling on edge.

- struggling to concentrate.

- going blank during interactions.

Unfortunately, GAD doesn't just affect people mentally. Over time, it also begins to take a toll on one's physical body; therefore, you can expect physical symptoms to include

- diarrhea

- fatigue

- irritability

- suffering from irritable bowel syndrome (IBS)

- muscle aches or tension

- nervousness

- nausea

- sweating

- trembling

With GAD, you won't feel a sense of worry every minute of the day, but anxiety continues to consume even when there's no reason for it. So, sometimes, you may find yourself feeling anxious about the safety of you or your loved ones, despite there being no trigger for it. You may also find yourself feeling anxious over believing that something unfortunate is about to come your way. While it may seem pretty harmless at first, a prolonged habit of entertaining such ideas will cause you a lot of distress, especially when you're in a social setting. It may even begin to affect your career and the relationships you have with others.

If you find yourself worrying so much that it starts affecting the overall quality of your life, including feeling so irritable and depressed that it pushes you to resort to alcohol or drugs or having suicidal thoughts or behaviors, it may be a good idea to seek professional help immediately. Negative thought patterns like these aren't likely to go away with time, and by not addressing them, you risk worsening them over time. So, living with GAD can prove to be a challenge in the long run, and it usually comes with other disorders like mood changes. Most times, people can manage the disorder with psychotherapy or medication, but lifestyle changes, relaxation techniques, and coping skills may work in your favor as well.

Depression

If you find yourself endlessly trapped in feelings of sadness and hopelessness, this may point to a mental illness called depression. In addition to your fatalistic view of life, you also find yourself experiencing a lack of interest, appetite, energy, concentration, and sleep. When it's left unattended, some people resort to self-harm and suicide, as it brings up emotional and physical issues that affect how people operate at home and at work. This is because the condition affects how you feel, think, and behave; however, with more people and institutions learning about depression and its effect on people, research, medical, and scientific efforts have made it possible for serious illnesses like depression to be treatable.

Like any other illness, depression will affect each person differently, and this means anyone can find themselves suffering from mild to severe symptoms, including

- always feeling sad and hopeless.

- constantly feeling guilty or worthless.

- no longer finding any pleasure in activities you used to enjoy.

- struggling to concentrate, think, or make sober-minded decisions.

- gaining or losing weight due to changes in appetite.

- struggling to commit to a proper sleep routine.

- entertaining thoughts in line with suicide and death.

- engaging in meaningless habits like pacing up and down or handwriting.

- experiencing a change in speech and movements.

At times, certain life experiences, like heartbreak from ending a relationship or the loss of a loved one, will leave us in a state of hopelessness. It's then that many people use the term depressed pretty loosely, and it's important to note that depression is different from these forms of sadness or grief. Yes, certain experiences will be a lot harder to work through than others, but it's expected that someone will grieve the death of a loved one or feel heartbroken from a relationship that didn't turn out as planned.

When you're dealing with depression, however, the negative thoughts and emotions don't change over time. In other words, depressed individuals won't find themselves feeling positive one moment and negative in the next. Instead, all pleasurable desires will decrease, and this will be accompanied by intense feelings of self-resentment and worthlessness. It's in moments like these that an individual may want to end their life because they feel they're undeserving of it and cannot cope with the feelings of complete hopelessness. Of course, traumatic and hurtful experiences can lead someone to depression; however, it's important to know what's identifiable as grief, sadness, and depression. Like mistaking a fever for an infection, not distinguishing between these terms may lead to people not receiving the right assistance and treatment.

Unfortunately, regardless of your demographics, depression can affect virtually anyone, and factors like biochemistry, personality, genetics, and environmental issues can all play a role in leading a person to a state of depression. Fortunately, with the help of a health professional, you can go through a physical examination and interview that will help evaluate your condition and possibly diagnose you with a mood disorder. Should you be found to be suffering from depression, you'll be placed on treatment that may involve medication, psychotherapy, and ECT.

There are also self-help coping mechanisms that you can adopt to reduce your symptoms of depression. Regular exercise, a healthy diet, and quality sleep have proven to be highly effective in creating positive thinking habits, thus improving one's mood. With different ways to help address and manage depression, you have the option to choose a plan that you know will work for you in the best way possible. For this reason, people have no excuse to ignore or leave their condition unattended, as this can worsen personal situations. This means that choosing to "give yourself time" won't improve your condition in the future, such as when people hope a new romantic relationship or better-paying job will improve how they feel and think about their present situation.

Examples of Negative Thinking Patterns

We usually imagine that negative thought patterns show up as sudden outbursts, panic attacks, pessimism, or always having bad things to say about ourselves. While these are all external examples that we see from people who have a negative and unhealthy mindset, the terror doesn't end just there. In addition to the negative thoughts, voices, emotions, and patterns that are going on internally, these thoughts, voices, emotions, and patterns are intensifying with time. In other words, something that started as a small seed of anxiety, worry, rumination, self-worthlessness, self-criticism, and obsession over problems will eventually grow into many of the examples that we're now about to discuss.

What the Fruit Now Looks Like

We spent a bit of time discussing what happens when you take a low-vigor seed and allow it to germinate into a fruit. You should have a general idea of how we would expect someone to behave when they feel stressed, anxious, and depressed, but it's important to have a clear understanding of what truly happens when you entertain negative thought patterns for a long time.

Polarization or Dichotomous Thinking

In life, it's sometimes necessary to find a gray area in situations and people, as this allows you the opportunity to confront situations from a more understanding and empathetic perspective, since you put the rules to one side and address things more humanely. As we grow older and learn how tricky and complicated situations and relationships can get, it becomes a challenge to simply view things from a black-and-white point of view. Think of a self-defense case. You have a perpetrator who attacks their victim, and while this happens, the victim is unable to leave the scene for one reason or the other. With the perpetrator still determined to achieve their goal, the victim is left with no choice but to resort to self-defense.

By looking at this as black and white, the victim is seen as wrong for causing harm to the perpetrator, since we live in a society where any sort of violence and assault is generally against the law. In an oversimplified situation, the perpetrator and victim will both be prosecuted and charged accordingly without the victim receiving any kind of leniency or understanding as to why they were left to respond the way they did. Sound practical, just, or realistic to you? Well, neither does it seem that way to me and many others who believe in seeing things from a gray point of view.

Many of the situations and relationships we're placed in do and will require us to use a gray lens if we value compassion and empathy, since we all make mistakes and offend others, both intentionally and unintentionally. However, to have the courtesy of compassion, empathy, and understanding applied to us, we need to exercise these values to the people around us so they are also extended to us in our times of need.

When we entertain negative thought patterns, we adopt dichotomous thinking patterns that oversimplify complex situations, making them black or white, good or bad, yes or no. It's an all-or-nothing mentality that we adopt because when we're so critical of ourselves and feel worthless, we do all we can to make no room for compromise or mistakes. In your mind, you strive to always be the best because, to you, your value and definition of success depend on it. As you may have gathered by now, this is an exceptionally dangerous way of thinking, since one's success, confidence, and worth shouldn't be tied to the number of wins they achieve.

Emotional Reasoning

We engage in emotional reasoning when we use our feelings to explain and justify causes or ideas that we support, even when this reasoning goes against facts. Somewhat similar to how we view individuals who are said to be stubborn or hard-headed, you often find yourself feeling like you're hitting a brick wall when you try to engage with, much less change the mind of, someone who has adopted this way of thinking. This is because people who use emotional reasoning center all their thoughts and emotions on negativity and apply zero logic or rationality to what they believe. Most times, they remain passionate and adamant about making those around them understand or feel the very same way, since they're constantly building narratives to support their own ideas.

Overgeneralization

How many times have you come across a man or woman who once went through a tough breakup and is carrying a lot of trust issues because they now believe that "all men or women are the same?" Like the many people who have similarly overblown ideas about every other man or woman in this world, there are just as many people who also have overgeneralized ideas about other life situations.

Overgeneralization occurs when you take one specific negative experience or detail and use that to judge future experiences, since this one factor now carries great significance in your life. Not only does it cloud your judgment, but it also stops you from truly giving your all in situations and relationships that are yet to come.

Labeling

Another example of a negative thought pattern is placing negative labels on yourself, your situations, your environment, and the people around you. Think of the embarrassing moments many people have in grocery stores when they head over to someone who appears to work there, get a quick greeting, and then proceed to ask their question without taking a moment to politely ask if the person works in the store. Many people make assumptions based on certain attire or energy, when in fact they are mistaken. Or think of the times when a crusty young man approached you unexpectedly and you immediately assumed they were a thief. These are all because of the ideas we form in our minds that we later impose on situations and people around us without being conscious of what we're doing.

In the same light, when you establish negative ideas about yourself in your head about being a loser, useless, stupid, or unqualified, these ideas impose themselves on how you think and behave in the future. As a result, these negative perceptions will become the new you.

Jumping to Conclusions

It's normal to find yourself innocently jumping to conclusions from time to time. We find this happening quite a lot in romantic relationships, like when we start coming up with odd ideas after we find our partners accepting calls from "Hannah" or "Tom" at odd hours of the evening. Later we find out that these individuals are simply the new assistant or co-worker that our partners are working with on an important project. Of course, jumping to conclusions becomes a problem when we assume that those around us are plotting against us, thinking the worst, or aware of something we haven't yet revealed. Not only does this encourage a habit of trying to read the minds of others, but it affects how you treat yourself and others in events to come.

Let's say you reach out to a close friend one day and notice that they've read your message but aren't responding. You monitor their social media activity throughout the day and catch them logging in and out of their account from time to time. Even after reaching out to them again, they still don't respond, and you now begin to suspect the worst. With no explanation as to why they're not responding to your messages, your mind begins to entertain thoughts, like maybe they're ignoring you on purpose, you've done something wrong, they're in danger, or something has happened but they just don't have the guts to tell you. Now let's assume it's the next day and you're attending an event that they will also be attending. Assuming they ignored you on purpose makes you change your behavior toward them. And by ignoring or behaving strangely toward them, they also pick up on that energy and start to respond in the same way.

It could be that your friend had accidentally opened your message the first time and planned to respond to you a little later, since they were busy during the day. That does happen; however, by jumping to conclusions and responding accordingly, you risk creating even more tense energy toward others, since the assumptions you make are only centered around negative ideas.

Mental Filtering

When you find yourself among individuals who make a habit of pointing out your wrongs as often as they can while never acknowledging the things you get right, this is known as mental filtering. Here, the person makes a conscious or sometimes unconscious decision to record every negative part of an individual or situation. As an outsider looking in, this is when you'll find yourself dealing with an individual who treats you or others that way. As someone who does the actual mental filtering, you may find yourself unable to acknowledge, focus, or praise any of your achievements because you only make mental records of your failures.

Overanalyzing and Indecisiveness

By adopting negative thought patterns, you may find it challenging to become decisive about small and big matters because you allow several factors to influence your decision even when you're well aware of what you want. A good example of this is when you find sales agents approaching you with deals and packages that they believe will be of interest to you. By already knowing you have no intention of purchasing the product, you've made a conscious decision of what you want to do; however, because the sales agent has spent more than five minutes explaining and convincing you to invest, you start to feel guilty at the thought of breaking the disappointing news to them because "they've spent so much of their time trying to get you to buy." So, you make the unwanted decision to buy even when you know you had no intention to do so.

It's good to be considerate toward others in what you believe is their "time of need"; however, once your consideration starts to encourage you to commit to things you weren't planning to, this becomes unhealthy. It's important to not dwell too much on making other people's issues your own because, at times, you're simply seeing things that don't necessarily exist. What if the sales agent had already met their target earlier that day and only approached you because you seemed like someone who would be interested. You assuming they're in need only places you in an uncomfortable and unplanned situation.

In all you do, consider the options that only concern you, take your time, and find polite ways to say "no" in situations that will require you to do so when making a decision. Avoid obsessing over your well-thought-out decisions because it's no use to say no to the sales agent only to later find yourself feeling guilty about your decision. Afford yourself the time you need to make a sober-minded decision, make that decision, and stick to it.

Negative Rumination About Past Events

As we already discussed earlier in the chapter, making an effort to reflect on how you respond to situations and allow experiences to affect you is healthy. However, spending unusual amounts of time dwelling on your faults and weaknesses isn't healthy, especially if a large amount of time has gone by without you having come up with any solution to the problem or way of moving past it. To keep you away from pondering over negative ruminating relating to your past, try finding meaningful ways to become more present. This includes taking time to invest in any challenges, interests, or projects that you may have. This will not only take you away from dwelling on the past but also help put things into perspective for you.

Outward-Directed Anger

Many of us have once been victims of ill-treatment, whether it's from a bully at school, a friend, a relative, or a stranger. Like labeling, we tend to keep the negative encounters we had with that one person and use them in judging anyone else who shares similar traits or qualities as that person. For example, people who have had bad encounters with a police officer at some point in their lives will likely respond in an aggressive, withdrawn, or rude way to any other police officer that they meet in the future. This is only because they are redirecting all the anger they felt in an experience to someone that they feel is similar.

To help you with this, you can always use your gray lens to try and understand the next person from their perspective. If you're justified in behaving how you did, then using the gray lens won't necessarily mean you were wrong for having a response to the situation. Instead, placing yourself in another person's shoes will bring you the answers and understanding that you were hoping for. In doing so, this will also help you establish a healthier and more effective way of dealing with people like that.

Fear of the Future

After explaining what anxiety is and how it affects an individual, it's easy to create a close link between anxiety and fear, since they're often used interchangeably. However, in this context, there is a difference between the two.

It's important to remember that anxiety is often about uncertainties concerning the past and future. This means that in the case of it being about the past, you ponder over situations that have already happened but remain unsure of what the outcome would have been if your response had been different. In the case of it being about the future, you go over situations that are yet to come but develop a restless anticipation toward the event because you're unsure of what the outcome will be.

When it comes to fear, it becomes different from anxiety because instead of developing uneasiness and nervousness over uncertainty, your negative emotions are now about feeling as though what you're hoping for is out of reach. This means that even though you are sure of what's to come, you still have negative thoughts about there being a possible change somewhere along the line. This is an unrealistic way of thinking because no one knows what the future holds. Therefore, by investing your emotional energy into something you're pretty limited in changing, this thinking pattern won't assist you in any way.

Negative Self-Criticism

Criticizing yourself is both a cause and an example of negative thinking habits because although there's always room for improvement in working on our weaknesses and polishing our strengths, negative criticism doesn't offer you any sort of constrictive or meaningful solution to any of your issues. Instead, it paralyzes you, making you feel trapped and unable to take hold of any of the experiences happening in your life. So, in a bid to work on improving yourself in every capacity, adopt a balanced way of viewing your achievements and character instead of obsessing over qualities and mistakes that you're working on improving.

Lack of Self-Confidence

We've already discussed the different elements that give rise to a lack of self-confidence, and we mustn't limit this concept to not being able to stand up for yourself, shying away from social settings, or not finding yourself attractive enough to others. Its impact does a lot more than that in the sense that you're unable to approach or confront situations, dreams, or challenges head-on because you don't feel deserving or worthy enough. So, reminding yourself of who you are, affording yourself the credit you deserve, and allowing yourself to get a fresh perspective will help boost your confidence and change the way you think and feel about yourself.

Habits That Lead to Cognitive Distortion

Think about your hands, feet, and other parts of your body. The fact that you can physically see what they can do makes physical control over our bodies far easier to imagine and do. However, when you think of thoughts and emotions that you can't physically see, it becomes almost impossible to imagine any sort of control that you can have over them. For this reason, most people don't concern themselves much with investing in their mental well-being, and instead, poor decision-making and bad behavior are blamed on what different people and environments have done to them. Developing a positive mindset takes a lot of work and time; however, it's doable. With that said, entertaining negative thought patterns and not choosing to explore solution-oriented ideas is ultimately a choice, and by settling, practicing, and making this a regular tendency, it becomes a habit.

When something goes on long enough to become a habit, the ideas you once thought were little and harmless turn into things that are a lot bigger than they were initially. This is what happens when you reach a point of experiencing cognitive distortion. By making a habit of entertaining negative thought patterns, the fruit of what once appeared to be a little and harmless seed is now magnified to the point of irrationality and exaggeration. In other words, your way of thinking now becomes inaccurate and faulty enough to influence how you understand yourself and everything that's going on around you. So, let's look at three habits that, when done long enough, will eventually lead to cognitive distortion.

Overthinking

Let's say you and a few friends have decided to go for a walk tomorrow, and they've left it to you to decide which park you'll all be heading to. With three different parks to choose from, it's normal to be a little undecided on which park to go for. But decision-making processes become unhealthy when it's no longer just about which park has the best walking trails. Your thoughts start taking over, like: "I saw a video of a lady being attacked by a vicious dog the other day. What if there's one on the loose at the park?" or "Lucy got seriously hit by a car last week. What if I get bumped by a bicycle while on the trail with my friends?" or "A news report just announced there is a serial killer on the loose. What if the serial killer unexpectedly attacks me?"

The vicious dog, bicycle accident, and serial killer on the loose are all thoughts that will eventually spark fear, anxiety, and stress within you. When you entertain unhealthy thought ideas long enough to trigger doubt and insecure emotions, this is known as overthinking. Simply put, it involves looking at a task that's been handed to you and doing all you can to think and model all the worst outcomes that could occur while handling it.

When overthinking becomes a habit, you find yourself applying the thought pattern to every decision that you need to make—big and small. Not only is it time-consuming but it's also draining because you find yourself constantly coming out looking silly and irrational when none of the events you found yourself obsessing over turned out to be true.

If you feel your overthinking is uncontrollable, take steps to deal with it by limiting the amount of time you spend entertaining a thought. And with every decision that's left for you to make, give yourself a deadline for how long you feel you should take to make a decision. But be realistic and practical in doing this. If the good decisions you made in the past took about an hour for you to think about, avoid pressuring yourself to a five-minute deadline. In addition to this, you can make time to participate in activities like yoga, breathing exercises, and other physical activity so you can use physical effort to relieve any unhealthy tension, anxiety, and stress that you may have.

Rumination

By now, you should understand that rumination is a cyclical negative thought pattern that allows your past mistakes and weaknesses to influence what you believe about yourself and/or the future. You may believe that things are only going to get worse because you aren't worthy or don't deserve good things in your life. This works against the objective behind self-reflection and self-improvement because your mind is clouded with a negative mindset that makes you feel stuck and helpless.

Like every other cause of negative thinking, only you have the power to stop and change this way of thinking. You can always seek professional help to assist you in working through this challenging time of your life, but as a start, you can use constructive hobbies like reading, taking a walk, or talking to close friends to keep you away from entertaining these negative thought patterns. But as you do this, be careful to not take up hobbies just so you can distract yourself. The point of a hobby is simply to take you away from fixating on an idea for a while, but not to forget it. It's your job to dig a little deeper and find what triggers lead you to feel this way about yourself. It will also help take you away from indulging in things like alcohol and food, which will only worsen the situation.

Cyclical Hostility

When you project your inner anger, judgment, and inability to trust others onto other people, this is known as cyclical hostility. Trauma and various insecurities play a big part in leading people to think this way, but when it's left untreated for too long, it starts to affect your ability to establish and keep any sort of support system in place because you believe people shouldn't be trusted; or worse, that they're also evil and dangerous.

Again, you can seek professional help to assist you in tackling this thought pattern. But in the meantime, exercising empathy can do a lot to help you break your cyclical hostility habits down. This will create instances where you place yourself in another person's shoes to view things from their perspective.

Breaking Negative Thinking Patterns

We're fortunate to live in a time when we're exposed to accessible resources, support groups, and free suggestions on lifestyle changes and habits that we can adopt to change our mindset and thought patterns. As you decide on the steps you take to adjust your thinking patterns and improve your overall life and well-being, there are simple practices that you can put in place to begin the process of setting yourself free from negative thought patterns.

Depression may make you feel like there's no longer any hope, solution, or freedom in where you are right now. But what many fail to understand is that, like the story with the glass of water in the teacher's hand, holding onto these negative emotions only leads you to feeling completely paralyzed. Since no one can take you out of that toxic space except you, it's up to you to adopt the right mindset and habits that you need to set yourself free. And because of the link that exists between your physical body and your mind, a mental transformation will improve your health by

- lessening your risk of health conditions such as hypertension, panic attacks, and high blood pressure.

- reducing your chances of suffering a heart attack.

- shifting you away from always falling sick to having a stronger immune system that is quick to respond to diseases and infections.

- improving your stress levels.

- improving your digestive system and ability to sleep better at night.

- giving you more zeal to do things like exercise.

- transforming your mood to being more optimistic, happy, and hopeful about the future.

So, let's get into the different ways you can go about breaking any negative thought patterns that you may have.

Scheduling Negative Thinking

With common sayings like "I can't control how this makes me feel," the idea of scheduling a thought may sound a little odd to many people, since a lot of us don't believe we have an ounce of control over how we feel or what we think. When you understand how the mind works, however, you can see the great influence that you have over it.

Make a deliberate attempt to set time aside to think about any negative thoughts and emotions that you may have. Granted, entertaining negative thoughts may not be of benefit to you and may worsen your mood; however, it isn't rational to avoid entertaining any negative thoughts at all. There's a way through everything, and you've yet to be exposed to people and environments that will rub off on you the wrong way. It isn't practical to shut that part of you down because when people and environments cause you to feel and respond a certain way, you can choose to attend to your negative emotions, reflect on what's happened, and find practical solutions to help you recover.

It's important to remember that negative thinking is normal. The problem is when it becomes a harmful habit that you can no longer control anymore. When you take a moment to think about what's going on in your mind, you ask yourself meaningful questions that will help you understand:

- What is the problem?

- How did I reach my mental conclusion?

- What are the steps that I can take to correct this thought?

By answering these three questions routinely, you spare yourself from dwelling on the problem or thought for way too long. Your mindset will change as you come up with a way forward for how to handle the situation. The point is to allow yourself to feel the way you feel and fully acknowledge those emotions instead of avoiding or stopping them. You're entitled to feel the way you do, as these are only human responses to situations; however, your response and how you process everything is what matters.

Replace Bad Thoughts

After scheduling your negative thoughts, avoid making the mistake of obsessing over the way forward. Let's say you get into a heated disagreement with a friend, and they go weeks without speaking to you. The issue clouds your mind each day, and you're struggling to move past what's happened. You then schedule your negative thoughts and reach the point of realizing what the actual problem is and how the two of you can move forward; you simply need to reach out first. Your decision to reach out may be the solution to your problem, but after sending that long-awaited text message and not seeing an immediate response, the waiting game only makes you anxious and restless about what's to come.

In the event that you've found a solution to your problem, replace any negative thoughts that you may have with positive ones as you wait to work on the problem or receive assistance or feedback . This will help keep you away from your usual cycle of fearing the worst and becoming anxious about what's to come.

Replacing a negative thought won't be easy, because negative thought patterns are pretty powerful; therefore, you need to make an intentional effort to undo and redo everything that's going on in your mind. This will require a great deal of repetition and practice.

Love Yourself

Self-criticism and feelings of worthlessness keep you from finding anything positive to believe and feel about yourself. You may feel overweight, unattractive, and useless for several reasons, but instead of beating yourself up about everything and speaking to yourself in a way that you would not repeat toward someone else, become your own best friend and give yourself the same advice that you'd expect from a loyal, honest, and caring friend. In this way, you'll be using the same compassion, encouragement, care, and love you'd expect from your best friends and family.

Journaling

Having evidence of your transformation can be very encouraging as you work on changing your negative thought patterns. One way you can do this is by journaling your negative thoughts, breaking them down, documenting your solutions, and returning to review the patterns and habits that you later changed to see the progress that you've made. In organizing your thoughts and analyzing them bit by bit, any progress that you make on your journey will make you feel positive and productive. It will also help you work through any future negative thoughts that you may not be aware of.

Be Honest With Yourself

Negative thought patterns and the defense mechanisms that you use to protect those thoughts are very complex and often challenging to work through. It's when you choose to improve your way of doing things that you then start to ask yourself the difficult questions that you may have been avoiding this entire time. As you truthfully sit down with yourself and look into all your negative thoughts and where different defense mechanisms come from, don't be too quick to rush yourself into having answers to every question that you may have. Instead, practice patience and understanding.

Exercise and Meditation

In every effort you make to change your negative thinking, remain intentional at all times. Once you realize the damaging impact negative thought patterns have on you, you may find yourself either stuck in the future, desperately wanting to see yourself having overcome this hardship, or trapped in the past when you finally get to the bottom of what led you to certain points. It's in moments like these that you should practice mindfulness because it allows you to be present and not obsess over the past or future.

Through meditation and exercise, you can practice mindfulness in becoming attentive and aware of all there is so you can center yourself mentally and achieve emotional and mental clarity. Those who find fulfillment in using physical activity to manage their negative thoughts and emotions will use exercise as a way to reach mindfulness. On the other hand, those who search for a sense of balance, peace, and calm to benefit their overall health and emotional well-being will find a lot of comfort in meditating as well. Choosing the right technique for you will depend on your preference; however, your efforts may prove to be a lot more meaningful if you participate in both exercise and meditation.

Chapter Summary

The gloomy, critical, or worrisome concepts that come to mind in response to particular circumstances, events, or experiences are known as negative thoughts. They may be habitual and deeply ingrained thought habits that affect our emotions, actions, and general well-being. It can be difficult to control negative thoughts, which frequently come to mind instinctively. They could be affected by present circumstances, worries, insecurities, or the past. Effective management of these automatic patterns depends on recognition. Negative emotions like sadness, worry, anger, or guilt can result from bad ideas. They establish a feedback loop whereby unfavorable emotions feed back on unfavorable thoughts and vice versa. It's important to question the truth of negative thoughts if you want to control them. This type of cognitive restructuring can aid in the development of a more impartial viewpoint.

Chapter 2:

Facing the Enemy Within by Identifying Your Negative Thoughts

When you often take things personally and assume different situations and responses are about you, you're unconsciously using these two things as a defense mechanism to protect what's going on inside you. Many of us make the mistake of thinking everyone in the outside world is against us and out to bring us down; however, hurtful situations, betrayal, disappointment, and offense are all a part of life for every living human being on this planet. So, while we're working so hard to control situations and what others think about us, we don't realize that the mess we're trying to cover up or fix on the outside is really the mess that lives on the inside. We're just unaware of how much effort we're putting into ensuring "nobody knows."

Unfortunately, the enemy you're looking for in your friends, close family, colleagues, and strangers doesn't live anywhere but within you. Granted, patterns like polarization, emotional reasoning, overgeneralization, labeling, jumping to conclusions, and mental filtering are examples of negative thinking, but have you ever wondered why we lean on them so much? We use them to protect ourselves from situations that we have already peeled, chopped, cooked and served in our heads. But while we think we're protecting ourselves from what may come, we're really guarding internal flaws and weaknesses that we don't want anyone to know about. So, to work through our negative thinking, we need to identify the enemy so we can understand it and deal with it.

Jumping to Conclusions

We've already established that jumping to conclusions means using insufficient information to make premature decisions. This can be in a positive, negative, or neutral way. For example, it's something like assuming someone isn't happy with you simply because they ignored your text message or didn't wave back when you waved to them. Other than the worst-case scenario, there are many possible explanations as to why certain outcomes turn out the way they do.

With a negative approach to jumping to conclusions, this thought pattern typically shows itself through casual assumptions, inference-observation confusion, fortune telling, mind reading, extreme extrapolation, overgeneralization, and labeling. But when it comes to the real reason why people think this way, it all comes down to our cognitive systems. Our capabilities and human skills are what make up our cognitive systems; therefore, this is the part of our brain that perceives, understands, concludes, and learns things *(Jumping to Conclusions: When People Decide Based on Insufficient Information – Effectiviology,* n.d.*)*. However, to achieve efficiency, we rely on mental shortcuts that we trigger to shorten the time it takes to make up our minds on something.

Various instances in life call for us to make decisions quickly; therefore, we often trigger this thought pattern, and this makes it into a natural thing to do. So although the idea of jumping to a conclusion does often have a negative connotation, it's something we often do because there are many instances in life when we need to make a quick decision, since the information at hand is limited. Therefore, this is a normal part of our lives, but it becomes unhealthy to do when we make negative observations and decisions that are likely associated with paranoia, anxiety, stress, depression, and fear. This means the thought patterns are only useful to us when we apply them to healthy situations that we can navigate reasonably.

By breaking the thought pattern up in this way, facing this enemy will entail

- always checking the facts.

- making it a point to challenge your thinking.

- asking questions if there's anything that is unclear to you.

- trying to view things from a different perspective.

Catastrophizing

Always thinking of the worst-case scenario and the most disastrous outcomes without real reason to do so is also a negative thought pattern that you can overcome. Common signs that come with catastrophizing situations include

- immediately feeling depressed, pessimistic, or anxious at the thought of an idea.

- feeling like all kinds of disastrous ideas are running through your mind.

- having a mental impasse.

- becoming overwhelmed with feelings of anger and fear.

- talking negatively about yourself.

- constantly searching the internet for solutions to your problem.

- overthinking every event, situation, or choice that you make.

Catastrophizing leads to all kinds of negative emotions because it makes you believe you don't deserve good things and that it's impossible to experience any form of positivity in your life. So, as a response to how you're feeling, you start looking for reasons that will support your negative ideas, since your goal is to avoid the reality that you're fearing. So, when it comes to why people think this way, research connects it to the following:

- **Depression**: Depression isn't only physically and mentally draining but it also brings a person to a point of feeling hopeless about their overall view of life. When you swim in this pool of negativity long enough, this leads to points of continuously imagining the worst-case scenario across different aspects and situations in your life.

- **Anxiety**: When our anxiety works to protect us from harmful and dangerous situations, it can be good for us, since we can use it to steer us in the right direction. But the minute it becomes uncontrollable, leading us to feel trapped and unable to live a normal life, that can ultimately lead to catastrophizing.

- **Interoceptive Sensitivity**: Interoceptive sensitivity applies to people who pay an abnormal amount of attention to their body and then exaggerate small changes that they notice. So, let's say they feel light movements in their stomach or believe their heart rate is beating faster or slower than usual; they will use these changes to call for some sort of action. It's when they make a habit of this that it leads them to catastrophize any sensations that they have in their body. *(What Is Catastrophizing? 6 Ways to Stop Catastrophic Thinking,* 2018*)*

Low self-esteem and fear can lead people to entertain ideas of catastrophe, but feeling unworthy or unable to handle situations and events doesn't mean there's no solution to the problem. To stop catastrophizing, you can consider the following techniques:

- journaling your thoughts to recognize patterns and monitor your journey of change

- putting mindfulness into practice

- developing the courage you need to face and challenge your fears and thoughts

- scheduling times to think over your worries and fears
- shifting your focus to solutions and not problems
- embracing the fact that there are situations that you'll have no control over
- brainstorming different solutions to problems that you feel may come up
- confiding in a close relative or friend about your thoughts

Overgeneralization

We understand overgeneralization to be a negative thought pattern that causes someone to take the outcome of an event and assume that every other event that's similar will produce the same outcome. Similar to how we'd understand people who walk around life carrying pain, resentment, and bitterness over individuals and experiences, people who overgeneralize things usually express their frustration and emotion in a destructive and damaging way. As a result, overgeneralization is caused by people who have suffered a previous trauma and have now concluded that they have every right to fear, avoid, and become anxious about future similar events. Therefore, in this case, you'll find yourself constantly

- imagining the worst outcome.
- believing sayings like "once bitten, twice shy," where you think that one failure should teach you a valuable lesson about future events.
- entertaining self-critical thoughts.
- thinking you can't do anything right.

- taking one event and connecting it to other patterns that you've also recently noticed.

But like anything in life, nothing is impossible. And despite the severe effects that come with overgeneralizing many things in your life, you can look into changing this thought pattern by

- looking into each conclusion's pros and cons.

- taking a thought and attempting to find several supporting facts that can prove your conclusion to be true.

- questioning whether or not others share the same sentiment as you.

- asking yourself if you'd come to the same conclusion if someone else shared the same experience and asked you to advise them on it.

- asking yourself if you aren't allowing your feelings to cloud your judgment.

- searching for instances that may prove your conclusion untrue.

Emotional Reasoning

We understand emotional reasoning to be an instance where an individual who experiences severe anxiety and panic attacks will become extremely dependent on their feelings and use them to guide their decisions. So, this will appear to people as

- feeling intense feelings without any evidence to justify them.

- making a mistake that you later regret saying or doing.

- assuming bad things will happen because of your current state of emotions.

- acting in a way that hurts both you and those around you as a result of your uncontrollable emotions.

Because anxiety is associated with feeling unsettled and restless because of the unknown, your brain starts finding ways to make sense of certain thoughts so you can ease your severe anxiety and reduce your chances of getting a panic attack. As we've already said, some people find themselves jumping to conclusions to find the answers they may be looking for, but in some cases, people also use emotional reasoning as a mental shortcut to get the answers they need.

When you entertain negative emotional reasoning, you're allowing your negative emotions to determine how you will judge and conclude a situation. Therefore, you can overcome this with three simple techniques that we've already discussed:

- mindfulness

- journaling

- meditation

Labeling

We all have weaknesses, and we've all done things we aren't proud of in life. We may have made some poor choices or in some instances, behaved inappropriately. Like how many people attach a stigma to a convicted criminal and treat them accordingly, we often pose judgment and harshness toward ourselves whenever we think of our past mistakes, flaws, and weaknesses in a negative way. When we reach the point of labeling ourselves, this is caused by our mental habits of undermining ourselves, highlighting every significant and insignificant mistake and weakness that we have. We call ourselves names that will ultimately undermine our abilities. So, we can imagine this to look like

- using bad labels to limit your potential.

- believing that your ideas and behaviors are what make you useless because "only useless people think that way."

- often experiencing feelings of unhappiness and annoyance without realizing that your thought patterns have led you to feel this way.

- experiencing physical symptoms like stomach aches, headaches, panic attacks, and motion sickness.

- adding to your anxiety and depression.

In overcoming the negative labels that you have about yourself, healing begins when you no longer allow them to stick. Like regular labels and price tags, this may be challenging to do, since it's pretty hard to detach yourself from negative labeling. However, you can overcome this by remembering the following:

- You cannot be confined to a single definition.

- There's always room to change or improve anything about yourself that you may not like.

- You deserve a break.

- You don't need to strive to be perfect—just better.

- The thoughts you have about yourself ultimately influence how you'll live your life.

- The labels you give to yourself later become who you are.

- You cannot be placed in a category because you're a being with the potential to do more for yourself and those around you.

- Your words are powerful enough to be used.

- Experiences that don't kill you only make you stronger.

Chapter Summary

Understanding and efficiently regulating your negative thoughts begins with identifying them. Negative emotions frequently result from negative thinking. Be mindful of your emotional responses, since they may point to underlying unhealthy thought habits. Spend some time contemplating yourself and your life. Pay close attention to your ideas throughout the day but especially when faced with difficult situations. Keep an eye out for any persistent negative thought patterns. When you become aware of your negative thoughts, you may begin to challenge and reframe them. Replace unbalanced, pessimistic, and negative thinking with balanced, realistic, and uplifting thoughts. Your holistic health can benefit from this cognitive remodeling process, which can also result in a more upbeat outlook. Consider getting expert support from a mental health professional if you discover that unfavorable thoughts are significantly distressing you or having an impact on your daily life. They can provide advice catered to your unique requirements and situation.

Chapter 3:

Reshaping Your Mind by Replacing the Negative Thoughts

If we take the time to be a little realistic for a second, years of speaking down on ourselves and believing the world is against us won't go away with just a few days of standing in the mirror and telling ourselves we're useful, attractive, or smart. It also won't become any more believable if you find yourself going from "Man, I'm so useless" to "Man, I'm so useful," either. This means that it's not enough to simply read up on a definition and think, *That's me.* Change will only happen when you make a consistent and intentional effort to figure out how exactly you identify with certain thought patterns. When you get to the bottom of what negative things you tell yourself, which experiences made you feel worthless and undeserving, why certain things make sense to you in a certain way, and what things you overgeneralize, this will guide you to where change needs to begin.

If you see yourself identifying with certain symptoms, it's not enough that you agree with these points and issue a diagnosis. If you've concluded that you tend to overgeneralize things, ask the question, "What single event have I gone through that's led me to strongly believe future events of a similar nature will produce the same outcome?" Was it a past relationship that disappointed you? Was it a traumatic experience that you went through? What exactly are you overgeneralizing, and what led you to that conclusion?

Introducing BLUE and TRUE Thoughts

To reshape your mind, you need to change your thoughts, but the symptoms and definitions you'll find in this book or on Google won't show you exactly what is going on in your mind. Yes, we can explain your thought pattern, tell you what's caused it, and provide you with the solution, but this is only a general view of your situation. For change to occur, you need to know what exactly you're thinking so you can get to the root cause of it, affirm it into a positive thought, heal, and then stop it in its tracks whenever you find it creeping up on you in the future. So, let's get into identifying these exact thoughts.

BLUE Thoughts

When we talk about "BLUE" thoughts, we're talking about thoughts that involve

- blaming yourself.
- looking for anything bad and not positive.
- unhappy guessing.
- exaggerating situations in a negative way. *(*Morin, n.d.*)*

In a nutshell, these "BLUE" thoughts are a representation of all the negative thoughts you have that are too negative to be true.

Blaming Yourself

Owning the part you play in a situation is a healthy way of taking accountability for your actions. However, when taking accountability for your actions turns into excessive self-blame, this becomes a problem. Again, it all comes down to what you find yourself doing with the thought. If all you're doing is pondering over the fact that "you ruined everything" and "it's all your fault," this isn't taking you anywhere. On the other hand, if you acknowledge your part and focus on what you can do in the future to not make the same mistake, this is more constructive.

Looking for Anything Bad and Not Positive

A teacher once walked up to a student with a clean white paper that had a single small dot in the center of the page. When he got to the student, he asked him, "What do you see?" Instead of saying he saw a white sheet of paper, the student squinted his eyes while staring at the small little dot in the center of the page and answered, "I see a small black dot."

Like the students, many of us make a habit of zooming in on the bad, even when it's only a small aspect of our lives. Of course, this is not to undermine the influence that negative experiences can have on a person; however, change often occurs when we shift our focus from the small black dot to the large white paper. Yes, it's good to reflect on our mistakes, weaknesses, and areas of our lives that we feel need improvement, but not to the extent that we undermine ourselves and our capabilities. It's only to establish a sense of balance in our lives, because assuming you're perfect, always right, and untouchable is also not a helpful way of life.

Unhappy Guessing

We all have some idea of what will happen tomorrow or in the days to come. These ideas can either make you feel hopeful and excited or helpless and gloomy about what's to come. Happy guessing would involve you feeling hopeful and excited about what the future has in store for you. But unhappy guessing will leave you imagining all kinds of unpleasant instances, like failing a test, not believing you'll qualify for a position you recently applied for, and thinking your relationship won't last longer than three months. When you tell yourself these things long enough, the thoughts that you have about the outside world will begin to satisfy the negative thoughts you have going on inside.

Exaggerating Situations in a Negative Way

Exaggerating a situation means turning a pimple into a mountain. If you gain a few pounds after not attending the gym for a few weeks or panic so much in an interview that you ask for a quick break and that the interviewer repeat the question, you might negatively exaggerate the situation. You might begin to think you're a loser because you haven't been following your fitness plan, or assuming you've ruined your entire interview simply because you felt a little overwhelmed.

With this way of thinking, you place yourself on a pedestal of striving for perfection and success at all times. Here, there's no room for any mistake, and even in natural or expected instances, you beat yourself up about things you feel you should've had more control over. This only worsens the way you feel and takes you away from thinking the matter through realistically and humanely.

TRUE Thoughts

We use TRUE thoughts to replace our BLUE thoughts. With TRUE thoughts, the goal is to take any BLUE thought that you may be having and ask yourself, "What advice would I give a close friend of mine who came to me with the same problem or thought?" So, let's say you one day find yourself thinking, *I'll never get that job because it's too good for me.* Because it's a negative thought, you're going to leave it there and allow it to live in your mind rent-free. But TRUE thoughts require you to ask yourself, "What advice would I give a close friend of mine who came to me with the same problem or thought?" This not only encourages you to exercise a bit of compassion and kindness toward yourself but it also encourages you to work on a solution to your problem. Therefore, when you think, *I'd tell my friend to consider getting a qualification for the job just to increase their chances of getting the job*, you're indirectly coming up with a solution to your own problem.

TRUE thoughts don't exist to "make you feel good." They're there to remind us of realistic ideas we should be entertaining in the event of us feeling a negative way. Remember that negative thoughts trap us in a pool of feeling hopeless and stuck. So, it's natural to desire a promotion at work, but it's also normal to admit to yourself that you don't presently meet all the job's requirements. Negative thought patterns keep you in that pool of despair; however, a positive mindset brings up possible solutions, like listing some things you can do to improve your chances of landing the job.

Practical Ways to Reshape Your Negative Thoughts

Even if you often have a pessimistic way of viewing things, the decision to reshape your thoughts is possible with consistency and a plan to be intentional about your journey. According to research, it takes 21 days for an individual to form a habit (O'Brien, 2020). With the 21/90 rule, it takes a person 21 days to form a habit and 90 days to turn that habit into a permanent way of life. Therefore, by training your brain and mind to change its focus onto more positive thoughts, over time, this way of thinking will become natural, and the view you'll have of yourself and your capabilities will transform into something more realistic and meaningful. So, let's look at some practical techniques that you can apply to reshape your way of thinking.

The Two-Column Technique

The two-column technique is an exercise or method that helps you assess your negative thoughts more precisely. To do this, you'll need to follow these steps:

1. Take a piece of paper and split it into two columns.

2. In the left column, list all your negative thoughts without overthinking them.

3. In the right column, list one to three positive points of view to every negative thought on the list.

Remember that because negative thought patterns are made up of denial, unrealistic self-criticisms, and incorrect assumptions, centering yourself back to where you should be will require you to see things as they are and not as you *think* they are. By consciously opposing every one of your negative thoughts with a realistic point of view, this will set you free from any negative outlooks that may have been trapping you this entire time.

As you put this technique into practice, avoid thinking too much. Write the negative thought down as it is in your mind and if other thoughts pop up along the way, write those down, too. The more you do this, the more your mind will begin to distance itself from your inner critic, and over time, these negative thoughts will change.

New Evidence

Negative thought patterns are unhealthy, and despite their inability to produce any constructive outcome, the ideas you have about yourself and your surroundings are based on some kind of evidence. So, people who see themselves as large will eventually believe they are because they see their physical bodies the same as others who consider themselves "fat.". People who see themselves as unattractive will eventually believe they are when multiple people tell them so. Even if this evidence is untrue or insufficient, all that matters is that a negative thought will always stem from something. People don't wake up one morning feeling fat, unattractive, unworthy, undeserving, or incapable of doing anything right. All these thoughts are fueled by something or someone.

While reshaping your thoughts, your new thoughts have to be believable for change to occur. And to make them believable, you have to present these new thoughts with new evidence. Otherwise, your efforts will be just as fruitless as an overweight person looking in the mirror each day and saying they're skinny just so it's believable. Your mind won't believe that for as long as there's no evidence to support it.

By gaining new evidence to feed our minds, we're adopting valuable knowledge about ourselves and the world through experience. And once this new evidence becomes believable to you, your mind starts to think your new beliefs are true. So, to make this exercise simple, let's start by getting you to set an alarm each day for the same time. When the alarm goes off, get up, look in the mirror, and immediately list five positive things that you love and value about yourself and your achievements. If you can do this long enough, you'll apply the same technique to every other individual and situation around you each time a negative thought starts creeping up on you.

Self-Compassion

To establish a healthy connection with yourself, you must cultivate self-compassion. This means no longer beating yourself up about situations. Here, the moment that a BLUE thought arises, you immediately take a step back and realize that it's your inner critic at work again. But you have a choice—you're either going to take the inner voice as a warning about real danger, or dismiss it if you find that it's your inner thoughts simply judging you again.

Be kind to yourself by exercising self-compassion. Remember that feelings like anxiety and fear can help keep us from harm because it's often our instinct that warns us about possible dangers. When you're able to detach yourself from self-criticism and self-doubt, you allow these negative emotions to do what they're supposed to in warning and protecting you when the situation calls for it. So, instead of striving to stop negative thoughts altogether, detach yourself from the ones that won't add any value to your life. This will keep you balanced.

Socratic Questions

When you aren't sure of whether how you're processing something is healthy, ask yourself Socratic questions like the following:

- Would I speak this aloud to another person?

- Would I tell a youngster this?

- Would I allow someone to address me in such a manner?

Self-Acceptance

As cliché as this may sound, it's important to accept yourself for who you are, especially when it makes you authentic. In areas of your life where you realize that certain habits and lifestyle choices don't better you as a person, you can work on those habits and choices to bring you closer to being the best version of yourself. The same goes if you desire to further your studies or get a better job. None of these decisions are coming from a perspective of hate. You cannot expect to produce admirable qualities and achievements for yourself when all of that's been fueled by ridicule, hatred, or any kind of negative emotion. Bad seeds cannot produce good fruit. So, in light of your wanting to change certain things about yourself, start by embracing your starting point to continue showing yourself love along the way.

When you don't accept yourself, guilt grows on top of the negative thoughts that you already have. Your suffering can become greater as a result of the resistance this creates to your current experience. Recognize any unfavorable thoughts that come to mind, and after pausing to realize them, make every effort to push them away. This doesn't mean internalizing the concept but instead allowing it to escape by writing it down, journaling about it, tearing it up, disintegrating it, and discarding it. It's normal to not always have the drive or stamina to fight against these ideas every time.

Chapter Summary

Your mental health and attitude on life can be greatly enhanced by replacing negative thoughts with more uplifting and helpful ones. Be aware of your thoughts and recognize any negative thought patterns as they appear. The first step in confronting and replacing unfavorable beliefs is awareness. Engage in activities that make you happy and satisfied. Your mood can be improved and bad thoughts can be diminished by engaging in hobbies, spending time with loved ones, or doing activities you are good at. Be kind and understanding to yourself like you would to a friend going through a difficult time. Be kind to yourself and work on your self-compassion. Instead of concentrating on issues, focus your efforts on identifying workable solutions. Negativity and feelings of helplessness can be lessened by becoming proactive.

Chapter 4:

Be Your Own Best Friend

Part of reshaping your negative thought patterns involves becoming your own best friend. However, before we get into how exactly you can do that, we need to understand what a true friend is. When we have a clear idea of what a true friend is, we can then use those qualities to adopt them for ourselves.

We establish friendships based on finding people with whom we share similar values, hobbies, behavioral patterns, and habits. The actual desire for friendship forms when we feel we can be comfortable, open, and vulnerable in their presence. In some cases, the relationship can exist to offer you and the other person a healthy support system in the physical, emotional, mental, spiritual, and sometimes financial aspects of your lives. A friendship like this will be based on qualities like the following:

- loyalty
- empathy
- honesty
- trust
- forgiveness
- acceptance
- support
- listening

- kindness
- respect
- care
- generosity
- dependability
- love
- integrity

When we talk about becoming our own best friend, this means making an intentional effort to find the qualities we'd typically desire in a friend in ourselves. It means being the support you need within yourself so you're able to watch over yourself like a friend on the outside. They would never betray or make you feel low and unworthy for any of your weaknesses and mistakes.

Apart from helping you overcome your negative thought patterns, becoming your own best friend will help you value yourself enough to walk away from unpleasant, uncaring, harmful, and fruitless relationships. When you can be all you need for yourself, you avoid instances of needing to seek validation and approval from others. It happens that we sometimes find ourselves in social circles and situations that don't add any value or meaning to our lives. When you long for a true friendship, you go to great lengths to prove yourself, and it's when others don't reciprocate the care, support, and validation you offer that you look within and start entertaining negative thoughts that make you feel worthless and undeserving. By having the friend you need already living within you, you fill the void of loneliness and desire to feel accepted.

Life will often come with situations that will leave you disappointed, hurt, angry, heartbroken, and overwhelmed. This will be the case even when you overcome your negative thought patterns. When these situations generate negative feelings within you, you should be able to rely on the friend within you for the approval, support, love, protection, humor, and inspiration that you need. Here, reassurance is key, because life will have you questioning yourself from time to time. This will create a lot of self-doubt, so being able to correct these negative thoughts without needing to ask for help from others will help reshape your mindset. Your relationships shouldn't be what is responsible for improving the way you think or feel about yourself.

The RAIN Technique

Because we grow up being told to love and accept ourselves without being taught how to do so, many of us don't have a clue as to how to go about being content with who we are. Unfortunately, when we feel hurt and in pain, it's a lot easier to turn to feelings of worthlessness and dislike, since we don't have to go far to find ourselves feeling this way. It takes a lot more work to correct any negative thoughts that we have; each time life knocks us down harder and harder, our negative feelings grow stronger and stronger if we aren't aware of or confident in who we are.

If you're looking to reshape your thinking, the Recognize, Allow, Investigate, and Non-Identification (RAIN) technique is a practice that you can use to control your emotions, accept realities concerning yourself and those around you, and discover more about who you are (admin, 2018). Its job is to improve the relationship you have with yourself because it guides its learners on how to achieve their mental goals without blowing things out of proportion or needing to suppress their negative emotions. Let's break down each part in this practice:

- **Recognize**: Take the moment to recognize all the thoughts and emotions that are running through your mind. When you're unsure of how you're feeling, ask yourself questions that will help you break down the idea so you can finally identify it. When you recognize each one of your emotions, it's only then that you'll be able to regulate them. The reason most of our negative emotions intensify in an argument or situation that upsets us is that we're fighting with ourselves or those around us to get our points across. In other words, we're struggling to make ourselves or the people understand how we feel. When we immediately recognize how we feel, it's much easier to handle situations calmly because we will have already done the validating ourselves.

- **Allow**: Allowing yourself to feel the way you do is also part of accepting experiences as they are and not as you think. We often believe in only accepting what we want, like, and prefer, but sometimes, going against your desires may be what's necessary to accept situations for what they are. This is often evident in situations involving relationships. Granted, you may want the relationship to work out; however, it may be necessary to allow the relationship to fall apart so you can move on with your life and stop holding on to situations and people that are holding you back. Accepting the idea doesn't necessarily mean you will want, like, or prefer this path, but it may be necessary.

- **Investigate**: Ask yourself questions and try getting to the bottom of why you feel the way you do. While you do this, remember to answer questions like we've discussed in a compassionate and non-judgmental way in order not to fall back into negative thought patterns. The point of investigating your thoughts is not to trigger yourself but to develop a more intimate relationship with your inner being.

- **Non-Identification**: Always remember that your emotions don't define or control you. In other words, you should identify and accept what you're feeling without losing yourself in the process. A good example of this is when you make a mistake. Negative thought patterns make you believe that instead of making the mistake, you *are* the mistake. Distance yourself from experiences to know that you're only having the experience and aren't the experience, as this will help you develop an identity that's separate from what you are going through.

How to Become Your Own Best Friend

The RAIN technique is meant to help you work through your thoughts while showing yourself the compassion, care, and love that you need. So after recognizing, accepting, investigating, and separating yourself from each experience, it's time to envision an end goal that will align with you becoming your own best friend.

Get to Know Yourself

Part of becoming your own best friend means reassuring yourself in your time of need. To reassure yourself, you need to have an understanding of who you are, and to do that, you'll need to follow these steps:

1. Start by visualizing your ideal self.

2. Explore your passions.

3. Try new things.

4. Evaluate your skills.

5. Identify what you value about yourself.

Respond to Your Needs

When you're unable to pour into yourself, you rely on the help of others to do so. Part of building a relationship with yourself means fulfilling any need that you may have. Of course, having relationships outside of the one you have with yourself is valuable, but you shouldn't find yourself developing an unhealthy obsession with a friend, spouse, or relative simply because "you can't live life without them." If this is the case, you've made them responsible for your happiness, attention, reassurance, and validation, and this is unhealthy and unsustainable.

When you finally reach the point of wanting to learn to respond to your own personal needs, you'll do so by

- starting to tune into your body.

- pinpointing your needs.

- asking yourself questions about what you need.

- letting others know about what you need so they can support your efforts in building a relationship with yourself.

Understand That Being Your Own Best Friend Isn't an Act of Selfishness

When we think of a selfish individual, we automatically imagine someone who makes everything about them and hardly leaves any room for anyone else to matter. Imagine you have a piece of paper with a list of names of your loved ones written on it. When we're selfish, we picture the piece of paper as having only our name on it because according to us, being selfish means having everything revolve around us and us alone. This explains why many of us are made to feel a lot of shame and guilt when we're labeled as selfish, but there's a difference between being selfish and being a narcissist.

Selfishness means putting yourself first. So, in the case of the list, you'd list everyone you care about in order of who matters to you most, but on your list, you will remain number one. This is all about you realizing that you can put yourself first while also allowing room for others to matter to you. In becoming your own best friend, the person you believe should take priority in offering all the fulfillment you need is you, and you'll do this by

- being the best friend that you can be.

- watching your inner dialogue and correcting it.

- vowing to yourself that you'll stop telling yourself things that you'd never say out loud to the next person.

- showing yourself the support you need.

Engage in Self-Care

Contrary to popular belief, self-care isn't just about buying expensive items for yourself now and then. The act of spoiling yourself isn't limited to just that. When we talk about engaging in self-care, this means adopting practices that you know will either improve or preserve your well-being and overall health. In other words, you take responsibility for staying happy and go the extra mile for yourself.

When you get into discovering who you are, you'll learn about the different things that make you happy and help you feel good. This will help you grow an even stronger relationship with yourself because you won't rely on the actions or comments of others to make you feel good about yourself. Granted, receiving positive feedback regarding your efforts is satisfying; however, the downside of seeking this kind of approval from others and not yourself is that if someone you value doesn't show you any sort of appreciation or recognition, this affects you negatively, and that's when you begin entertaining thoughts in line with feeling worthless and undeserving. So, by giving yourself the approval, appreciation, and acknowledgment that you need through investing and rewarding yourself accordingly, you're able to remain in positive spirits regardless of what others say or think about you.

Fortunately, it doesn't take much to engage in self-care because you can always show yourself the approval you need by

- practicing mindfulness.

- being honest with yourself about your weaknesses.

- speaking sincere words of self-acceptance over yourself.

- choosing to forgive and self-forgive.

- knowing your values.

Be Honest With Yourself

Unless you choose to confide in someone else about your thoughts, no one else will know. Simply put, there's no need for you to lie to yourself about what goes on in your mind. While reshaping your mind, identifying and breaking down every negative thought is key. Therefore, you'd be doing yourself a great injustice if you made denial and dishonesty a habit. To prevent that, you can keep the following in mind each time you work on being honest about a negative thought:

- Be vulnerable.

- Reflect on your decisions.

- Picture your future.

- Develop self-awareness.

Chapter Summary

It takes work to develop self-compassion, self-awareness, and self-care, but being your own best friend starts with you. You should treat yourself with the same consideration that you would show to a good friend. During challenging times, be kind to yourself and refrain from self-criticism. Focus on learning and improving from mistakes rather than obsessing over them. Recognize your attributes, values, and convictions. You can make decisions that are more in line with your genuine desires and that bring you closer to fulfillment by getting to know yourself better. Be mindful of your internal discourse. Replace your negative or self-deprecating thoughts with uplifting ones. Challenge your limiting beliefs and keep in mind your values and abilities. Avoid comparing yourself to others because doing so might make you feel inadequate and self-conscious. Pay attention to your own progress and adventure.

Chapter 5:

Sweat Away the Negativity by Exercising to Fight Negative Thinking

We often spend months or even years cultivating negative thoughts in our minds. Therefore, it's impractical to assume that a few days or weeks of reshaping your thought patterns will bring about the change you're looking for. Of course, one can celebrate their daily milestones and possibly see change within a matter of weeks; however, in reshaping your negative thoughts into positive ones, you don't just want to eliminate all the bad stuff for the time being. You still have your whole life ahead of you, and this means you've yet to face other challenges and hurtful experiences along the way. This means you need to equip yourself with tools that you can use at any point in your life to face any jab that life may throw your way.

Since negative thoughts are known to be unhelpful and will likely leave us feeling stuck and hopeless, we can use thought exercises to break free from our patterns while improving our mental health. Here, the point is to gain complete control over what goes on in your mind. When we invest ourselves in thought exercises, we eventually break into our subconscious thoughts as well, and once we're able to gain control over that part of our minds, our efforts will become more fruitful in ultimately eliminating negative thinking patterns.

Understanding Thought Exercises

A thought exercise is designed to provide you with a different way to understand a specific experience. Outside of viewing the situation from your own perspective, discovering other ways of viewing the situation can turn out to be helpful and liberating. Thought exercises are often used by psychologists and other mental health professionals who deal with cases related to all kinds of negative thought patterns, and over the years, these exercises have proven to be highly effective and sustainable.

There are numerous thought exercises that anyone can try, and the great thing about these exercises is that if one method doesn't seem to work for you after some weeks, you can always try another one. Here, it's all about exploring different techniques to find something that will work specifically for you so you can improve your overall mental health. Also, thought patterns aren't a medical treatment. Instead, they're ideas that you'll use to see the world a little differently.

Fortunately, aside from helping you reshape your thoughts, thought exercises come with several benefits that are both effective and beneficial to all those who choose to practice them. Advantages include

- having a go-to thought exercise that you can always turn to to help you remain calm in any triggering moment.

- helping you reduce the length and intensity of an anxiety attack, even when you aren't combining it with any form of traditional therapy.

- being able to monitor any growth and changes that may be happening in your mental health journey when you're pairing your thought exercises with mental health apps.

- affording us the chance to modify our lives each time we become aware of our triggers and learn to be more mindful of them. (Break Negative Thinking with These 6 Mental Health Exercises, n.d.)

Thought Exercises That Will Boost Your Mental Health

When you feel stressed, depressed, anxious, fearful, or angry, use any of these thought exercises to help fight your negative thinking:

Self-Observation

Traditions involving spiritual awakening usually encourage some form of mindfulness or self-observation. Although it's practiced in most spiritual traditions, those who don't follow a specific spiritual journey can still gain a lot from such an exercise. Any time you start to feel anxiety, stress, or fear, you can investigate the underlying issue by using this exercise.

1. Immediately distance yourself from people or any setting that may distract you from sparing a moment for yourself.

2. Spare a few minutes to be alone.

3. Center yourself and pay attention to how every part of your body is feeling.

4. Make a detailed note of every one of your physical feelings.

5. Become conscious of what you're thinking by noting the different stressors that could be rushing through your head.

6. Categorize each one of your thoughts so you can break each one down bit by bit.

7. Take each thought and make a mental note of allowing and accepting it so you can reassure yourself that you've validated yourself in the best way possible.

8. Once you've acknowledged all the sensations in your mind and body, take a moment to calm yourself by releasing any tense muscles and reassuring yourself that you've addressed each thought and have let them go.

9. Do this until the negative thoughts and feelings have disappeared.

Thought exercises like self-observation help negative thinkers center themselves as they find their way toward stress relief. Essentially, anxiety exists to keep us safe when we're under attack and we need to either fight back or walk away from a situation. The moment we're away from a situation and are finally in a safe space, this allows us to focus on other important things, like our physical well-being. This explains why self-observation exercises are beneficial in helping you remain calm, grounded, and in the moment.

A Thought Record

We often experience negative thoughts and feelings that we're unable to identify and understand at first. When we keep a record of our thoughts, even in instances where we're unable to make out exactly what they are, time can help us make sense of certain symptoms over time. Nowadays, with the help of technology, we have numerous ways that we can record ourselves. Voice recordings, journal apps, virtual diaries, and traditional notebooks are all excellent examples of the different ways you can go about sharing your thoughts. The option you go for will simply depend on your needs and preferences. Plus, with online options, you're usually afforded a creative platform that will allow you to personalize your journaling space and make it cozy enough to keep drawing you in, so you're always keen on recording your thoughts.

As you go about recording your thoughts, don't shy away from being as detailed as you can be. After writing everything down, take a moment to analyze the thought so you're able to be mindful of it in the future. Make a habit of revisiting your recorded thoughts from time to time. As you do this, you'll notice a certain connection between all the events and thoughts that you continue to share. It's then that you'll pick up on patterns that you need to work on, and once you become solution-oriented, you'll find yourself overcoming these negative thoughts one by one.

Interrupting Anxious Thoughts

Unlike fear or anger, which rely on evidence and truth to overcome, anxiety is an emotion that you can always avoid by distracting yourself with something else. While it isn't always a good idea to use distractions as a way to overcome negative thoughts and emotions, distraction techniques can sometimes prove to be effective when you're dealing with an emotion like anxiety.

When we talk about distractions, people immediately imagine the use of alcohol, substances, or other addictions. These are what I refer to as destructive distractions. On the other hand, you have constructive distractions that offer people a good diversion to their problems. If you're looking to interrupt your anxious thoughts, a constructive distraction would involve the following:

1. Create a physical space for yourself that's free of any sounds, including music, audiobooks, or shows, and make sure you're far from anything that could distract you.

2. Start the exercise by tensing and relaxing various muscles so your focus can move away from the anxious thought while moving toward all the activity that's happening with your muscles.

3. As you focus on your muscle activity, slowly breathe in and out while consciously monitoring your efforts with each count.

4. Think of any negative thought that may come up during this time and fight it by identifying the thought out loud, telling yourself that you're no longer going to entertain it, and speaking an affirming message over it.

5. After confronting the negative thought, reward yourself with a satisfying task that may involve something like playing your favorite game on your phone, engaging in a yoga session, doing some cleaning, or watching a calming video. If you're not sure what you may find to be satisfying, try counting backward.

Cognitive Defusion

We use cognitive defusion exercises to look at our thoughts from the view of being an outsider looking in. When we do this, we automatically distance ourselves from what's going on in our minds, and this helps us detach from our thoughts to gain more clarity. Here are four different ways you can go about this:

- Use a silly voice to gain a different perspective on the thought.

- Imagine your thoughts as leaves floating along a river and visualize yourself approaching these leaves and later walking away from them so you view your thoughts as separate ideas from their main identity.

- Consciously label each one of your thoughts so you can treat them as individual ideas that you choose not to believe.

- Acknowledge your mind by thanking it for doing its job in warning and protecting you from potential harm.

Self-Compassion

Practicing self-compassion is another thought exercise that you can use to fight away all the negativity. Sometimes, the thoughts that lead us to points of anxiety can be overwhelming, and this can turn into a never-ending trap that constantly leaves you feeling unmotivated and miserable. To fight this off and overcome it, you can always practice self-compassion. Here, you'd allow your mind to take the position of a close friend by imagining what that person would say to you if you'd confided in them about the negative thoughts that were going on in your mind. The point of this exercise would be to allow yourself the comfort you need to make it through a negative thought so you're able to avoid the critical voice that you often use on yourself.

Something else you could do as a self-compassion thought exercise is get your hands on an old childhood photograph of yourself. Take a moment to focus on the image and while you do this, visualize yourself transferring all your thoughts to the child in the image. This will give your adult self the opportunity to receive the comfort and compassion that the child in the image deserves.

The Worry Tree

Worry trees are thought exercises that are most helpful to individuals who have a hard time moving away from constant worry. This may be because it's now compulsive and no longer an emotion that they can simply fight off with quick reassurance. With a worry tree, you're put in a position of making a conscious decision to either continue worrying about the situation that's running through your mind or find a way to occupy yourself with something else. So, picture a graphic flowchart in your mind, and at different points of the chart, start imagining yourself pasting questions like:

- What is worrying me so much?

- Do I have any sort of influence over the situation so I can achieve my ideal outcome?

- Is it possible to address the matter right now?

As you go about answering these questions, when you find yourself unable to change the outcome of a certain circumstance or fully answer a question, the tree will help guide you to the point of letting the thought and worry go. If something can be done about the situation you're worrying yourself about, then the same tree guide will help lead you to a solution. By using this thought exercise to help you fight off worrisome thoughts, you can avoid instances of ruminating over situations.

Additional Ways to Fight Negative Thinking

In conjunction with the thought exercises that we've just discussed, there are other activities and techniques that you can put in place to help you fight and overcome negative thinking effectively.

Write It Down

Make a habit of writing down any unfavorable ideas or views that you may have on a piece of paper. As you do this, avoid filtering any of your thoughts and rather focus your attention on jotting down the thoughts and ideas as they come to mind. Each time you consciously take a thought and transfer it onto a piece of paper, you're setting your mind free from the negative ideas that may be occupying your mind at the time. When there's no more room for new thoughts to occupy your mind, this will allow your mind to fill itself with more positive thoughts, since those ideas will be your new focus.

Focus On It

Each time you make a conscious effort to write your negative thoughts down on a piece of paper, spare yourself a moment to truly focus on the thought. Be aware of the different sensations and feelings that you get the moment you bring this thought to your attention. When you're able to pick up on these sensations, do all you can to track the part of your body that senses them. When you find it, describe the sensation, experience, emotion, and part of your body that it affects through a few words or a drawing.

Notice the Thought

After writing your thoughts down and taking the time you need to focus on them, it's time that you acknowledge your thoughts by recognizing them and noticing any physical responses that they may bring about. It's always important to make yourself aware of how certain thoughts make you feel. This will help you break the cycle of constantly running back to negative thinking each time a surprise comes up or things don't go as planned. As people, we often make the mistake of pondering only on bad thoughts in succession. Therefore, by noticing each thought one at a time, you become aware of what's clouding your mind. In a moment to yourself, you can then alter the thought before taking on the next negative idea that may be bothering you.

Question Your Thinking

Make an effort to monitor all your thoughts and patterns by asking yourself questions like these:

- How many times a day do I have these negative thoughts?

- Can I express this idea aloud to others?

- Am I benefiting in any way from this way of thinking?

- How does my self-critical language affect me?

Think Two for One

Lastly, make a habit of attaching two positive ideas to every negative thought that you may have. As you go about throwing two positive thoughts in the direction of each bad thought, remember to throw an optimistic concept that's plausible and practical. Just as with using new evidence to correct your thinking of the evidence you have in your mind right now, you need to use concepts and ideas that you believe when you're in your right mind and feeling optimistic. It won't work to throw just anything your way.

Chapter Summary

Exercise has the potential to be a potent tool for overcoming negative thinking and enhancing general mental health. Endorphins are released during physical activity, which also lowers stress and elevates mood. Exercises that increase heart rate and create feel-good brain chemicals, such as jogging, brisk walking, cycling, dancing, or swimming, can help counteract negative thoughts. Strength training can increase your self-assurance and sense of empowerment, which can help you combat negative self-perceptions. While not a typical physical activity, meditation can be a very effective strategy for controlling unfavorable thoughts. You can examine your thoughts without passing judgment on them and let them pass without becoming preoccupied with negativity by engaging in guided meditation or mindfulness practices. Finding activities you enjoy and can routinely include in your schedule is the key. Gaining the advantages of exercise for mental health requires consistency.

Chapter 6:

Unraveling the Mind by Defeating Negative Thinking With Communication

Self-talk does a lot to shape our minds; therefore, when we entertain negative thought patterns, we look down on ourselves because we allow doubt to undermine our talents and abilities. In the event of you constantly questioning yourself, you lean more toward obsessing over your weaknesses and flaws because of something known as the negativity bias. The negativity bias suggests that human beings often pay more attention to experiences that are more negative than neutral or positive ones. So, like the scenario with the student who focused on the small black dot on the large piece of paper, we're more inclined to allow one small negative experience to ruin or cloud every positive experience or thought that we may have in our minds. Although many may think that only negative thinkers operate this way, you'd be surprised to learn that people often notice negative criticism and feedback over constructive criticism and positive feedback, regardless of their mental health status.

When you obsess over negative self-talk long enough, this eventually becomes self-doubt, and over time, self-doubt leads to conditions like the imposter syndrome, where your mind is now locked into believing that your achievements aren't worth acknowledging because "it's not a big deal" and "anyone can do what I do." Here, you make a habit of undermining any success that you may achieve along your journey because you don't think much of yourself and your capabilities.

How Communication Can Reshape Your Self-Talk

Believe it or not, communication has the power to change what goes on in your mind. It's cartoons that usually showcase true examples of what goes on in our heads when we're trying to work through an idea internally, like having a devil and angel sitting on each shoulder. This is an illustration of what goes on in our minds because when we have an idea, an internal conversation begins where we have the little devil and angel going head to head over how best to process the idea.

When you imagine an individual communicating with themselves poorly or inappropriately, what do you see? Is someone slapping themself on the face each time they make a mistake? Or do you perhaps imagine someone heading to the mirror, looking at themselves dead in the face, and proceeding to shout and scream as loud as they possibly can? We often think communicating is us reacting outwardly; however, we also do a lot of communicating with ourselves internally.

There's rarely a moment in your day when you won't be running an internal dialogue with yourself. This is whether you're raging over what another driver is doing during traffic, picturing what your spouse could be up to when they're not answering their phone, debating whether or not what you intended to be a joke was a joke, or wondering what your friends are thinking about what you just posted on social media. You're always having an internal dialogue with yourself.

We may not always be conscious of our internal dialogue, but it's clear that we spend more time talking to ourselves than to others. And like any conversation that you'd have with the next person, your inner dialogue can be either motivating or demotivating. Either way, a constructive or destructive conversation will make or break you.

A Communication Breakdown

Negative thought patterns can stem from underlying processes happening within your brain when you communicate with yourself. We've all experienced how things can easily and quickly take a turn for the worse when we're in a heated argument with someone else, and things can escalate just as quickly when our inner dialogue is taking a turn for the worse.

When we're unable to communicate with others or ourselves, this results in a communication breakdown that usually leads to frustration and anger. When you carry around strong feelings like anger and frustration, this leads you to have an unhealthy and distanced relationship with yourself. So, let's look at the different reasons you might end up having a communication breakdown with yourself.

Unwanted Repetitive Patterns

Until someone brings it to your knowledge that you have actual conversations with yourself throughout the day, you won't necessarily be aware of this. So, while you go about your life going back and forth on one thing or the other, you may not be monitoring the different conversations you're having in your head.

By establishing that we do experience communication breakdowns with ourselves, one of the reasons this happens is that we're struggling to work through certain conversations with ourselves. But struggling to have a conversation with yourself won't necessarily look like you have two devils in your head who are screaming at each other for hours on end. This type of communication struggle could show up as you go back and forth about an idea. Because it's leaving you frustrated, angry, and uninterested, you choose to "walk away from the conversation" by blocking it or distracting yourself so you don't have to face it anymore.

The older we get, the more we realize that the adult conversations we're hoping to have with someone else may need to happen with ourselves. So, when you're faced with owning up to your actions or seeing things as they truly are, this can be a rather unpleasant experience to go through. The moment you become defensive or habitually unable to respond maturely to your thoughts, the other voice in you then starts to do the same in defending its point. When you're stuck in a loop of having a constant back and forth between your thoughts, like feeling stuck in the same loop with someone that you know, you begin to lose interest in wanting to have any sort of relationship with yourself. The constant inability to have an adult conversation within results in Unwanted Repetitive Patterns (URPs), which are one of the reasons you have a communication breakdown within.

To overcome URPs and establish a relationship with yourself through communication, you need to look within and identify the conversations that you don't necessarily like to have with yourself. Without trying to justify your actions, blame your patterns on the next person, or run away from this needed moment, ask yourself questions that may give rise to the underlying issue that you might have. In doing so, you become aware of the ideas you keep feeding your mind, and that's when you can step in to change the conversation and ultimately work on finding a way forward to the problem. By changing the conversation, you'll be able to change the outcome.

Destructive Communication

Destructive communication is another way we can invite a communication breakdown within ourselves. While growing up, our parents, teachers, friends, and other people we interacted with regularly all had a part to play in guiding us on who we are and what we mean to those around us. Whether those comments were constructive or destructive, each of those experiences had a part to play in how we see ourselves today when we define our purpose, develop an image of who we are, understand the world around us, and determine our confidence.

Each one of the labels we attach to ourselves will provide a lens that we'll use to define who we are. So, when these labels are negative, these destructive ideas become a part of our internal dialogue, and that keeps us away from wanting to establish any sort of meaningful conversation with ourselves.

Improving the Communication You Have With Yourself

The only way you will be able to form any kind of relationship with yourself is by choosing to communicate with yourself in a better, more conscious, and more intentional way. To build a healthy relationship with yourself, you need to first pay close attention to the conversations that you have in your mind. This will give you a clear picture of what you've been telling yourself this entire time, and each time you spot negative, unhealthy, or destructive thoughts that are bringing you down and taking you away from having a relationship with yourself or causing you to shut down, take corrective steps to adjust the conversation immediately into something more positive, healthy, and constructive. Also, try to pick up on any habitual patterns that constantly make it hard for you to have an adult conversation with yourself.

To increase your self-awareness and establish a relationship with yourself, you can always reassure yourself with these important reminders.

Focus on What You Are Feeling Right Now

If you're feeling down and flooded with negative emotions, allow yourself to focus and acknowledge these emotions. In doing so, don't allow these emotions to define you, because your low moments will dissipate at some point. The tricky part about negative thoughts, however, is that, unlike your feelings, these can be persistent and not want to move away from you until you choose to let them go. So, increase your self-awareness by paying close attention to your feelings.

Share Your Feelings With Someone Close to You

In trying to understand your feelings a little more, open up to someone close to you and tell them how you feel. As you do this, ensure you're calm and not emotional so you're able to pace and structure the conversation to be a fruitful one in the end. By speaking to someone mature and more experienced, you can get them to guide you on how to answer the different questions that you may have running in your head right now.

Treat Yourself

Treat yourself from time to time. You won't need thousands of dollars to do this. Depending on what you find to be calming and satisfying, you can always treat yourself to something meaningful, like a walk in a beautiful and peaceful park, calling a close friend, listening to your favorite music, or doing breathing exercises.

Take Time to Count Your Blessings

Gratitude can go a long way in helping you establish a relationship with yourself. You can always begin your journey of counting your blessings by being grateful for what's closest to you and taking time to either invest in yourself or be a blessing to others. Appreciating the special connections that you've formed with different family members and treasuring the experience that you've had at family get-togethers, celebrations, and special occasions can increase your desire to invest in yourself and those you value the most. It's all about being grateful for your efforts and the part that everyone else in your life had to play in building you to be who you are today.

Make Social Connections

Go out and enjoy the world! Live a little by going out to see a funny movie with a close friend who always leaves you in good spirits. If a friend, colleague, or someone you know is going through a rough patch, send them a motivating email or text message just reassuring them that all will be well soon. Also, work on finding a religious group or independent, structured social group that agrees with your philosophies.

Chapter Summary

By participating in positive self-talk and soliciting support from others, one can challenge and reframe negative beliefs to overcome them through dialogue. Talk to a therapist, family member, or trusted friend about your problems and your negative ideas. Discussing your emotions with others can help you obtain insight and support. Reach out to someone you trust and ask for their opinion if you're feeling overtaken by negative thoughts. A different viewpoint might occasionally offer a more impartial assessment of the circumstances. Isolation brought on by negative thinking can make it more difficult to counter those thoughts. Participate in social events and spend time with inspiring and encouraging people.

Chapter 7:

The Power of Compassion When You Find a Way to Serve

We can derive a lot of satisfaction from exercising compassion for others. When we're on the journey of transforming ourselves from within, we can't necessarily see the results of our efforts yet because exercising compassion within to change how you think and feel is a journey. But it helps to step out into the world to see the impact you have on others, as this will allow you to find a sense of purpose and gratitude for what you have and where you are in life.

Compassion is often undervalued and overlooked, but there's a lot you can take from showing deep sympathy for someone who's in a less fortunate position than yourself. It's often not enough to simply look at what goes on around you and think, "Shame." There's always something you can do to help the next person, and because you're on a journey of freeing yourself from your pains and suffering, you'll find a great deal of fulfillment from seeing someone else in need and taking an active step to alleviate their pain. Not everyone you help will be as appreciative as you may want. However, in the event of you making someone's day, putting a smile on a stranger's face, or getting that one needed hug, this can do wonders in changing the way you think and feel about yourself, especially if you've come to believe that you're worthless and undeserving.

You can feel a great sense of pain from watching someone else in need, but sympathy changes into compassion when you develop a strong desire to want to do something about that pain. You may already know yourself to be a compassionate person, but with an unhealthy thought pattern about who you are and how much you're worth, your compassion is likely either being taken for granted or overdone in the sense that you go out of your way to help others even when it's at your expense. So, you must have the right mindset when you do this to not have it work against you in the long run. Remember that your compassion isn't a weakness, and it should never be treated as one.

The Benefits of Exercising Compassion on Others

We've talked a lot about exercising compassion on yourself, but while you do this, do yourself a favor by exercising the same compassion on others. Here are some of the reasons and benefits that come with doing so.

Improves Your Physical and Mental Health

Compassion can do a lot to improve your physical and mental health. With you out and about volunteering in your community and interacting with others, this will allow you to explore different environments and learn new things. When you're constantly exposed to people who would do anything to be where you are or have what you have, this develops your sense of gratitude and over time, you'll become thankful for the big and little things that you have going on in your life, helping reduce any stress, depression, and anxiety that you may have.

With feelings of fulfillment and happiness now flooding your mind, you'll become more content with yourself and what you stand for. But feeling this way doesn't just benefit your mental health. Each time you feel this great sense of happiness and fulfillment within you, your body releases feel-good hormones like oxytocin. When you're constantly triggering yourself to feel this way, you'll eventually develop feelings of trust and love for yourself. And with time, these positive emotions will help you create a strong bond with yourself.

Strengthens Relationships

Although compassion can work against you when it's being abused by you or other people, it can also help cultivate healthy and strong relationships when it's being applied the right way. Each time we exercise compassion on the next person, this establishes a community among you and those you help. And when you're constantly in a position to help people, you strengthen any bonds and relationships that you may have formed along the way. You also gain a lot of trust from others because people who usually exercise compassion are kind, patient, understanding, and not quick to judge. They're also approachable and easy to connect with. As human beings, we're more inclined to open up and gravitate toward those who make us feel comfortable enough to be true to ourselves when we're around them. So, as more and more people start drawing toward you, you'll establish an intimate community of your own.

A Just Society

Negative thought patterns usually stem from us feeling violated in one way or the other. One of the benefits that come with exercising compassion is that being in spaces that allow you to help others affords you a break and breath of fresh air that's different from the people and environments that may be causing you to feel low and undeserving about yourself. In helping those around you, you do all you can to create the equitable and just society that you long for.

As we grow in showing compassion toward others, our efforts and visions start to change because we become more invested in ensuring that those we know are treated in a worthy and dignified way. So, when you're dealing with someone disadvantaged or less privileged than yourself, you develop a passion for ensuring that everyone around you has the support and resources they need to break free from their chains and struggles and thrive in any space or field they may choose to occupy. This is why people who support causes like these end up advocating for social justice. In doing so, they help promote laws and policies that work to identify different inequalities that exist within society and eliminate them.

Personal Growth

While you're on your journey of being kind and resourceful to others, you grow as a person and discover more things about yourself. Whether good or bad, having an already changing mindset will help shape you into being a better version of yourself. Always remember that we don't thrive in life because we only possess good qualities and strengths. Having flaws and weaknesses is a part of every single one of us; therefore, in identifying any weaknesses or qualities that you wish to change about yourself, you'll start to become conscious of the situations, people, and environments that lead you to become the worst version of yourself. By wanting to stay positive, improve, and grow as an individual, you'll begin to distance yourself from things that you know will bring out the worst in you. In showcasing more strengths and good qualities, this won't mean you no longer have weaknesses. It simply means you're aware of the spaces that trigger and do all you can to avoid them.

The more we exercise compassion, the more we learn to empathize and have a heart for others. In turn, this cultivates self-awareness, the ability to place ourselves in the shoes of others, and emotional intelligence. We also set ourselves free from all kinds of negative emotions that lead us to anger, resentment, and bitterness because we're gradually shifting our focus to things that truly matter and fulfill us in different ways.

Different Ways to Serve Others

Although we talk a lot about self-care, self-improvement, self-awareness, and learning to speak life and good things about yourself, you never know how much more you can achieve from doing the same for others. When you exercise compassion on yourself long enough, the effort will immediately extend to those around you naturally and effortlessly. But in waiting for it to pour out of you naturally, it's important that you also adopt hobbies that will cultivate this part of yourself even more. Otherwise, your negative thought patterns may find their way back to you time and time again, if you remember what the negativity bias is all about.

In connecting with others, building relationships, advocating for an equal and just society, and promoting personal well-being, the impact these efforts will have on you will surely turn out to be significant. Upon deciding to reach out to others and be a helping hand, always remember to participate and engage in activities that speak to you the most. This will keep you motivated and encouraged to keep going and continue to do more. By choosing to take up any activity that comes to mind without any thought, you'll find yourself dreading the experience within no time, and this could discourage you from wanting to give back to others entirely. So, in deciding what's most important to you, ask yourself the following questions:

- Which groups and causes are most important to me?
- What issues stir up a strong and intense feeling within me?
- Which organizations do I know will help me make the most of my commitment?
- Do the homeless speak to me, or can I showcase my compassion through arts?

Depending on your life experiences, these will motivate you to choose something that will help you create the reality you've always hoped for. Here are some more ideas that you can explore for giving back to those in need.

Donations

Donating doesn't mean you need to buy anything new to give back to the needy. There's always a lot you can do without even needing to give someone money or spend your own. You can always recycle old clothes, shoes, accessories, stationery, or items that you know will be of help to someone else. Ideas worth considering include

- selling items you no longer want or need at an affordable or free price.

- giving away any gadgets that you may no longer be using.

- keeping a spare jar around for any extra change that you hardly keep count of.

- donating any rewards that you won't be putting to good use.

- partnering with friends to keep giving more.

Feeding the Hungry

Many homeless people don't have any food sources to rely on for one reason or another. To make a difference, you can always

- give money to your local food bank.

- donate food to your local food pantry.

- hold a virtual food drive.

- volunteer with a local food bank.

Mentor

Someone can always learn a thing or two from you, and in building relationships with others, you'll gradually open up about your life experiences. Instead of blaming others for their life choices or dwelling on the past, consider mentoring those in a similar situation as yours. You may think your story isn't that significant, but in celebrating any milestone, big or small, share this with someone else and motivate them to also break free from any chains, habits, or patterns that could be keeping them from reaching their fullest potential. After doing this, put them up to a challenge by

- making them understand what you want out of the relationship.
- setting expectations together in the very beginning.
- showing sincere interest in their personality.
- developing trust.
- recognizing when to provide counsel.

Volunteer Your Services

If you're keen on playing an active role in your involvement with the community, you can show your passion by doing any of the following activities:

- serving the elderly in your neighborhood
- tutoring young people
- assisting the homeless, because homelessness is a global issue
- tidying up your neighborhood
- creating memorable holidays with others
- contributing your skills to fields that would benefit from your involvement

Brighten Someone's Day

Showing compassion to others doesn't have to be something you only do on weekends or family holidays. In the simplest of gestures, you can still brighten someone else's day in more than one way by

- sharing a compliment.

- picking up extra chores at home.

- paying the bills that day, week, or month.

- leaving kind notes.

- saying thank you.

- starting a conversation.

- giving unexpected gifts.

Chapter Summary

The strength of compassion rests in its capacity to profoundly improve not just our own lives but also the lives of others. We feel a stronger feeling of connection, excitement, and purpose when we practice compassion and look for ways to help others. Serving others doesn't require great gestures. Start small by lending a hand to a neighbor, working at a nearby nonprofit, or simply lending a sympathetic ear to someone in need. Look for neighborhood nonprofits or community organizations that share your interests. Volunteering your time and talents can benefit others greatly and also promote personal development and fulfillment. Perform random deeds of generosity without anticipating reward or recompense. Simple deeds like holding a door open for someone or sending a motivating message can have a big impact. Consider your service experiences carefully. Take note of the advantageous benefits it has for you as well as the recipients. You may be motivated to carry out and increase your actions of kindness after this reflection.

Chapter 8:

Harnessing the Power of Gratitude as a Shield Against Negative Thinking

Knowing someone in the world would do anything to be in your position and have what you have is a reality every one of us is aware of. And when we see a child or adult suffering, unable to meet their basic needs, or unable to do the very things we often take for granted, it's then that we take a second to think of how fortunate we are to have a job that pays the monthly bills or be able to take a walk thanks to fully functioning legs.

Because we're on the journey to transforming your thought patterns and adopting more positive ways of thinking, you have become more intentional about being grateful for everything you have and are capable of doing. Gratitude often does a lot to remind us that not all hope is lost, and this helps keep us in good spirits when we feel overwhelmed and flooded with thoughts that suggest everything is falling apart. But aside from that, gratitude also goes hand-in-hand with manifestation.

When we are grateful, we're immediately placing ourselves in a position of acknowledging that we are in a phase of abundance because we know that someone out there would do anything to be in the position we're in today. This is regardless of what you have going on at the moment. As soon as we enter the space of feeling like we're living in abundance, this sends positive vibrational messages to the universe. The universe obeys every instruction we give it; therefore, when we send it positive messages, it returns an outcome to us that's positive and in line with what we wanted in the first place. The only thing is that what we receive will always be larger than what we asked for. So, like the instance of the fruit and the seed, the fruit, which represents your outcome, will always be larger than the seed, which represents your input.

In cultivating gratitude as often as we can, the universe returns this to us in the form of more joy and peace. Therefore, you can use this knowledge to work in your favor by finding practically anything to be grateful for just so it's returned to you in greater abundance. In life, there will always be something worth being grateful for, and even in your lowest moments, remember the gifts of life, food, a roof over your head, a job, daily supplies, transport, opportunities, and the convenience of technology to be always thankful for something.

Different Ways to Cultivate a Habit of Gratitude

Depression can leave you in a pit of despair, hopelessness, and sadness for an indefinite amount of time. In overcoming this depressive state, you need a weapon that's strong enough to break you out of your trap and set you into a more positive headspace. Gratitude can be all the medication you need to give you the perception and strength you need to change your negative thought patterns into positive ones. Over time, your attitude and habit of finding practically everything to be grateful for will pour into other parts of your life, like your career, experiences, personality, social life, health, and relationships. So, instead of dwelling on what you don't have or where you could've been, your new focus will be on what you do have and where you are currently. Let's look at the different ways you can become more aware of your blessings.

Keep a Gratitude Journal

Make it a practice to remind yourself every day of the blessings, grace, privileges, and wonderful things you enjoy. You have the chance to weave a sustainable life theme of gratitude by setting aside time each day to reflect on your unique qualities and the people who love and care about you.

Remember the Bad

Keeping a record of where you're coming from isn't so you can dwell on it. Remembering your past struggles can help you be appreciative of where you are right now. This is because when you reflect on how tough life used to be and how far you have come, an explicit contrast is created in your mind. This contrast creates an environment that is conducive to gratitude.

Try to Notice When You Feel Grateful

Part of becoming more intentional about your efforts to appreciate all you have includes

- taking time to notice what's around you.
- practicing gratitude for the little things.
- sharing your gratitude for your loved ones.
- spreading gratitude via your social media platforms.

Consider Reflecting on What You're Grateful for

Avoid being grateful for possessions, positions, and experiences without giving them much thought. If you tell yourself that you're grateful for food to eat, reflect on why you're grateful for it. Perhaps you once went through a time in your life when you went to bed without eating that night. Or maybe you had a homeless person come to you today and ask for a bit of money just to buy something to eat. Why are you grateful for what you say you're grateful for? Ask yourself this question when it comes to

- more positive emotions.
- higher subjective happiness.
- higher satisfaction with one's life.
- fewer negative emotions.
- a decrease in symptoms of depression.

Smile More Often

It's simple to practice appreciation and positivity by smiling. That's because it can improve your mood and the moods of others around you. So, try to smile more often, even when you don't feel like it, and notice how your attitude and interactions with people change.

Chapter Summary

A strong approach to preventing negative thinking and encouraging a positive outlook is gratitude. When we are grateful, our attention is drawn to the things we already have and enjoy rather than the things we lack or are unhappy about. Gratitude aids in shifting our focus from unfavorable ideas to the positive aspects of our existence. We can lessen the effects of negative thinking by recognizing the positive things we have. When we express thanks, we awaken uplifting feelings like happiness, satisfaction, and appreciation. Positive attitudes and thoughts can balance out negative ones. According to studies, cultivating thankfulness can boost mental health by easing the symptoms of worry and despair. It is contagious to be grateful. When we start concentrating on the good things in our lives, we inevitably draw in more positive situations and ideas.

Chapter 9:

Write Down What You're Feeling

Movies tend to set a trend among teenagers by inspiring them to share their thoughts in a journal. To them, a journal, which we know as a diary, represents that one close friend who holds your deepest secrets, always listens, and never judges no matter what you tell them. You'd then seal it with a little lock or hide it under a mattress to ensure no one finds it or can open it.

Few of us keep diaries when we're older, and I guess that's because we hardly have the time to document every little detail that's going on in our lives. Just the thought of where you'd even start is a mission of its own. Also, many of us become a little paranoid in imagining what would happen if someone found our diaries because that would mean having someone look into our heads, which is something many of us don't want to happen.

Journaling can be a great way to eliminate any kind of negative thinking because it allows you to gather your thoughts and share your actual struggles and fears while being aware of them at the same time. With a tight lock or secret hiding place for your journal, you can make your confessions without fearing that you'll be punished or judged in any way. A practical way to vent your thoughts and emotions will help clear your head so you can get all the clutter out of it.

You may be wondering what the difference is between owning a diary and having a journal, but there's no clear difference. The term diary is used when we're referring to the book a teenager will use to write their thoughts, and the term journal is used when we're referring to the book an adult would use to share their thoughts. Essentially, the whole purpose behind journaling is to share your feelings and thoughts so you can understand them better. In knowing that they don't serve anyone else but you, your journaling efforts should be intentional and rewarding as you work on dealing with negative emotions like stress, anxiety, and depression. Over time, this will help you control your emotions a lot more while improving your overall mental health.

People are always advised against trying to ignore or suppress overwhelming emotions because you'll gradually become a ticking time bomb as you bottle all your feelings up and delay addressing them. Instead of avoiding them, you should find healthier ways to express them, and this is one of the benefits that come with journaling. In addition to acting as a meaningful tool to help you manage your mental health, it also offers benefits like helping you manage, cope, and reduce anxiety, stress, and depression.

Because our negative emotions are also linked to the moods we set ourselves in, journaling helps improve your mood by

- guiding you on how to prioritize any concerns, problems, or fears that you may have.
- monitoring any day-to-day symptoms that could assist you in identifying triggers so you can later learn how to control them.
- creating room for encouraging self-talk to help you recognize negative behaviors and thoughts.

Instead of keeping thoughts in your mind and spending time working through each idea one by one, write them down so you're conscious of them and can look into what's causing you to think or feel the way you do. There are many times when we may even forget certain important thoughts that need addressing, and by journaling everything, you're also able to keep a record of all your thoughts.

While journaling does come with many mental health benefits, getting the best results will mean partnering it with other lifestyle choices and habits that will also help manage your anxiety, fear, stress, and depression. This includes

- taking moments to relax and meditate each day.
- adopting a balanced and healthy diet plan.

- getting as much quality sleep as you can.
- avoiding possible distractions like alcohol and drugs.

How to Begin and Sustain Your Journaling Habit

Not everyone took an interest in keeping a diary when they were younger, but not having done so before doesn't mean you can't learn how to do it now! Here are ways that you can begin and sustain a journey in regular journaling.

Commit to Writing Every Day

A habit is a repetitive behavior over time. Simply schedule some time to complete your journal. You can decide to keep a bullet notebook every day first thing in the morning, right before bed, or even during your lunch break. Some people find that setting aside a specific time each day helps them keep up with a goal. But it's not necessary to journal at the same time every day, and you can do it at any time of the day. At the end of the day, use a routine that will work best for you.

Arrange a Time and Possibly a Location for Journaling

You can journal anywhere that feels like a quiet, effective location for your daily writing activity, such as

- in a comfortable chair and side table.
- while leaning back in bed and using pillows.
- sitting on a porch or taking a bath.

Set a Time Limit

Set a goal if you think it will be difficult to find the time to journal. Maybe at first, you can only commit to writing for 5 or 10 minutes each day. As you get more accustomed to the technique, work your way up to 15 or 20 minutes or longer. It is better to use a straightforward bullet journal. If being flexible works better for you, make that work. This is because schedules and formats may work well for certain people, but not everyone is a fan.

It's quite acceptable if you don't require or want a set location or time to journal. In that situation, don't limit yourself by insisting that you write in your journal in a specific location. Be willing to fit in your journaling whenever and wherever it fits into your schedule, whether it is hectic or organized.

Be Flexible

Journals can be creative, verbose, full of ideas at random, bulleted lists, or any mix of these. There isn't a single, best approach to journaling. Go ahead and do whatever you want; if you want to draw one day, write a paragraph the next, and make a to-do list the next. Above all, don't stress about what you're writing, especially in the beginning.

Chapter Summary

A potent method for reducing negativity and enhancing emotional well-being is writing down your feelings. You can let out repressed feelings and thoughts by writing. It offers a secure, confidential setting where you can openly express your emotions without worrying about being judged. Putting your feelings and thoughts into words aids in your understanding and helps you obtain clarity. It can reveal trends, catalysts, and root causes of negativity. Writing gives you a healthy outlet for your frustrations as opposed to letting them stew inside. By doing this, you can keep pesky ideas from taking over your head and harming your general well-being. Writing about your feelings might help you feel more in control of your emotions while also reducing stress. Writing helps you become aware of negative thought patterns so you may question and reframe them more successfully.

Chapter 10:

Embracing Change by Building New Habits to Combat Negative Thinking

By now, you should have a clear and willing desire to reshape and change your thinking patterns. Now that you understand negative thought patterns, know what causes them, and have learned how to overcome them, what do you now have to look forward to? In other words, what will your end goal look like?

What Embracing Change Can Do for You

In embracing this new change, you open yourself up to watching a powerful and positive impact take place in your life. This includes eight specific highlights.

Growth in All Aspects of Your Life

People fear change because it makes them uncomfortable, since change takes us out of our comfort zones. In not influencing what will happen when change comes, we're forced to open ourselves up to learning and doing something new. When we learn new things and do more, we grow, and this improves our strengths, skills, and capabilities.

Adaptability and Flexibility

Comfort invites routine because once we're able to predict outcomes and how things are done, we feel a sense of confidence and security. The ironic thing about adaptability is that although we gravitate toward wanting security to fuel our confidence, growing in adaptability means exposing ourselves to new situations that will ultimately change how things look for us right now. In being unable to adapt to change, we become insecure, stressed, and vulnerable. When we embrace change, we increase our adaptability to new people, environments, and circumstances. And because embracing change is a strength, we then look for opportunities to improve and advance ourselves in the process.

Validation and Re-evaluation

We walk into life with ideas, beliefs, and opinions that we use to shape how we see things. Although this does sometimes give you a narrow view of life, using this formula can influence your life when you come across someone with a view that's different enough to make you want to change your own. Some people will agree with your ideas, which is great in validating your points; however, those with a different opinion may cause you to want to reassess your life and reshape your views or the ideas and goals that you're supporting.

Exposing Your Strengths

Your reaction to certain life changes will expose the stuff you're truly made of. Especially when you feel like you're being backed into a corner, you'll surprise yourself in coming to learn that you had strengths hidden inside you that you never knew about.

Lessons and Failures

Doing the same thing all the time may offer you security and routine, but it won't create any room for you to grow or change. Through failure, we develop life lessons, and it's failures and lessons that lead us to success. The more open we are to change, the more experiences we have to learn from, and the more we'll get out of our situations.

The Guts to Achieve More

Practice doesn't make perfect. It makes it *permanent*. The more we do something, the better we get at it, so each time we're faced with a challenging environment or situation, it's the uncertainties, discomfort, and anxiety that give us the confidence we need when we finally choose to overcome it. Over time, situations will become a little easier to handle. Change can often be challenging to work through, but the beautiful thing about it is that it allows you to conquer your fears. This will help you generate an exciting anticipation for advancements and opportunities that are yet to come. And with more confidence and change, you'll start accomplishing all your goals.

Handling Setbacks and Appreciating Success

Challenges, setbacks, and hiccups are all a part of life, and part of maturing in life means not expecting everything to go as planned. When you're able to embrace change, this simply means that you'll maintain your neutral or positive attitude regardless of the outcome of a situation. You'll always have the mindset that something good and positive can stem from any situation. It's when we achieve success amid our adversities that we find fulfillment.

Different Ways You Can Work on Embracing Change

Embracing change doesn't mean always being the one in the passenger seat. Simply put, you don't have to wait for others to initiate change in your life to start finding ways to embrace it. By adopting new techniques and habits in your life to improve your thought patterns, you'll create the change you need and automatically begin to embrace it. So, let's look at the different ways you can go about doing that.

Examples of Good Habits

Habits you should now adopt to reshape your thinking include

- flossing your teeth at least once a day.
- getting at least eight hours of sleep every night.
- doing 10 to 15 push-ups a day.
- expressing your gratitude to your loved ones.
- eating fruits and vegetables every day.
- staying on top of grooming and bathing.
- drinking plenty of water throughout the day.
- practicing meditation or breathing exercises.

Write Down Your Goals

Always remember that journaling is key. First, make a list of your professional and personal objectives. To accomplish these objectives, new habits will need to be formed, so you must be clear on what they are. Now, pick a single objective and consider the routines you'll need to develop to achieve it.

Build Good Habits Into Your Routine

Go out of your way to

- set small goals.
- Lay out a plan for your life.
- be consistent with your time.
- be prepared.
- make it fun.

Reflect on Your Habits

Consider how your new habit is working for you as you continue to practice it. If you're finding it difficult to follow through, consider why. Think about motivating yourself by choosing a more attainable short-term goal. Consider what went wrong if your new habit isn't bringing about the change you were hoping for. To ensure that your habit is producing lasting change, you might need to make some adjustments.

Develop Self-Discipline

You can work on your level of self-discipline by doing the following:

- find your motivation
- identify obstacles
- replace old habits
- monitor your progress

Chapter Summary

Creating new routines to counteract negative ideas can be a life-changing process that gives you the power to take charge of your thinking and emotional health. To prevent overloading yourself, concentrate on just one or two habits at once. The possibility of success is increased and momentum is created for larger improvements by starting small. Create a weekly or daily schedule that includes your good practices. It takes consistency to implement long-lasting change. Celebrate and acknowledge your successes as you establish new behaviors. Any milestone that is celebrated, no matter how modest, encourages improved behavior. It takes time to develop new habits, and failures are common. Even if progress is slow, be kind to yourself and continue to stay dedicated to your objectives.

Chapter 11:

Mastering the Art of Self-Affirmation

Positive self-affirmations are phrases we say out loud to ourselves or write down in a bid to make them more real. Here, the point is to affirm them as often as you can so they can work to build you up and improve your overall self-confidence. Regardless of the positive or negative experience that you're going through, positive affirmations can help you overcome any negative thought pattern, especially when it's in line with self-doubt. Therefore, when you do this daily, you'll start minimizing all the negativity that's going on in your head and start seeing things in a more positive light.

It isn't always necessary to repeat the same phrase time and time again. The point is just to ensure that you're affirming yourself as often as you need to. When it comes to the benefits that we associate with positive affirmations, we can expect this regular habit to

- help reduce stress.
- improve your overall well-being.
- improve your academic performance.
- encourage you to be open to changes in behavior.

Using Positive Affirmations

Let's have a look at the different ways you can practice positive self-affirmations.

How to Use Positive Affirmations

You can use self-affirmations in any sort of situation or event. This includes putting the practice in play

- before presentations or key meetings to boost your confidence.
- during moments of feeling flooded with negative emotions like impatience, rage, or frustration that need to be managed.
- to boost your self-confidence.
- to complete the tasks you've begun.
- to increase your output.
- to get rid of an undesirable habit.

Set Them in the Present

Affirmations and objectives don't precisely work the same way, despite appearances to the contrary. Affirmations are used to assist in altering ingrained patterns and beliefs. Act as though you've already achieved success as a means of bringing about this shift. You have to keep working toward your objective. A positive affirmation, on the other hand, increases your self-assurance by highlighting your existing abilities.

Avoid Stock Affirmations

You can use an affirmation you came across and found to be particularly meaningful, but you might find that coming up with one that is especially suited to your objectives works best. Use your imagination and think of ways to make your affirmation as particular as you can give those affirmations can be about anything. Linking affirmations to guiding principles like kindness, honesty, or dedication is beneficial for many people. This can assist you in keeping your attention on the bigger picture of what matters to you the most.

Keep It Real

When you focus your affirmations on particular attributes or improvements you'd like to make to those traits, they tend to be most effective. Although change is always possible, certain adjustments are easier to make than others. Affirmations don't always result in change, and they may have little impact if they center on something you don't believe to be true.

Practice Affirming Yourself Every Day

As you go about making a daily habit of practicing self-affirmations, remember to keep the following in mind:

- Do at least twice daily; begin with three to five minutes.
- Each affirmation should be said 10 times.
- Enlist the assistance of a loved one you can trust.
- Make your routine consistent.
- Be patient.

Chapter Summary

Self-affirmations are an effective method for overcoming negative thoughts and developing a more upbeat and self-assured mindset. They entail purposefully speaking kindly of yourself, your skills, and your value. By substituting empowering and uplifting beliefs for unhelpful ones, self-affirmations challenge and rewire unhelpful mental patterns. These fresh ways of thinking eventually become second nature and can offset negative thinking. Having confidence in your abilities and strengths can help. When you have confidence in yourself, you are better able to face obstacles and failures with a more upbeat attitude. By encouraging positive self-talk, self-affirmations promote self-compassion. Self-compassion is a powerful tool for lowering judgment and self-criticism. With self-affirmations, you turn your attention away from your flaws and onto your strengths. This shift in perspective may lessen the tendency to dwell on unfavorable ideas. Self-affirmations are a useful tool for cultivating a cheerful and upbeat mindset. This may result in a happier attitude toward life and increased general well-being.

Chapter 12:

Mindfulness and Beyond— Empowering Your Mind With Meditation

In every effort that you make to improve your thinking patterns, being intentional is one of the most important things that you can do for yourself. Through mindfulness, you're able to center yourself in that very specific moment, so you're conscious and aware of everything that's happening within and around you. You achieve mindfulness through meditation, and by opening yourself up to doing this regularly, you can learn how to manage and master stress, anxiety, depression, and many other serious illnesses that you may be dealing with.

Many people who practice mindfulness talk about their increased ability to remain calm in the most uncomfortable situations, and with the improved self-esteem and confidence one develops over time, this positivity later becomes the sense of feeling more enthusiastic about what lies ahead. With control over our emotions, we're able to invest ourselves in more meaningful relationships while establishing quality relationships along the way. Therefore, by paying attention to your body and thoughts, you can achieve a lot in your life.

Different Ways to Practice Mindfulness and Meditation

Here are some great ideas for how you can go about practicing mindfulness and meditation most beneficially and effectively.

Let Your Body Relax

When we have negative ideas, we physically tense up, which heightens our degree of distress. In the event of this happening, give yourself a break from reality and take a few minutes to sit, breathe, and relax. Any part of your body that is feeling tense should be relaxed as much as possible. As you exhale, let the force of your breath relieve the tension and picture yourself sending it in the direction of the sore spot. While in meditation, keep your body still and mentally examine it from head to toe. Concerning your center of gravity, feel each component as you go.

Focus on Pleasure and Not Pain

If you have chronic pain or headaches, there is always something you can focus on that is based in pleasure. Consider how your body is feeling right now rather than focusing on your various ailments. If you're having issues, try rotating your shoulders, extending your neck, or doing yoga. You should begin to feel soft throughout your entire body, allowing you to focus your attention there.

Gently Observe Your Negative Thoughts

When a terrible thought strikes, resist the need to make it disappear. This is comparable to swimming with the current as opposed to against it. Instead, accept it as it is and watch it. Put yourself in the position of an observer rather than a thinker. Simply allow the idea to pass, remembering that you and your Higher Self are not responsible for your thoughts. Recognizing your negative thoughts will often be enough to break the loop before it starts.

Breathe Deep

When we are worried, we start to breathe more shallowly, which shows that we are not obtaining enough oxygen deep in our lungs. Pull your shoulders back, maintain a straight spine, and focus on taking many calm, deep breaths. If you find that your thoughts are drifting into negative patterns, you may educate your mind to pay attention to events that are happening rather than your ideas by bringing your focus back to the breath.

Meditate at the Same Time Every Day

If you incorporate meditation into your habits, it can become ingrained in your daily life. Although you don't have to meditate at the same time every day, teaching yourself to do so in the morning or right before bed will help you develop the habit far more quickly. Attempt to follow these procedures, even if it's just for a little while each day, to truly relax your body from the worry. As your confidence grows and you develop the ability to block out unfavorable thoughts, you will notice a shift in your attitude.

Chapter Summary

Positive thinking is fostered, and general well-being promoted, through meditation. Mindfulness techniques, which help you become more in tune with your thoughts and emotions without passing judgment, are frequently incorporated into meditation. With this knowledge, you can identify destructive thought patterns and shift your attention to ideas that are helpful and constructive. Stress and anxiety levels can be decreased by regular meditation. It is simpler to let go of negative thoughts and adopt a more positive view by soothing the mind and relaxing the body. Through improved emotional control, meditation can help people manage difficult circumstances with more clarity and optimism. You gain a deeper awareness of yourself through meditation, including your thought patterns, triggers, and reactions. You can make deliberate decisions to nurture positivity thanks to this self-awareness.

Conclusion

Even if you've spent years of your life stuck with negative thought patterns, it's never too late to reshape your thinking and produce a different outcome to your thoughts and feelings. One of the beautiful things about personal transformation is that it's a journey that you can gradually ease into, and with enough dedication and consistency, you will watch your life unfold right before your eyes in a positive and meaningful way. Regardless of your circumstances, remember that *you're* responsible for ensuring your lawn is clutter-free at all times. By leaving the job to those who hurt or disappoint you, you risk waiting for a change or apology that will never come.

People who have a hard time controlling the ideas that are flooding their minds often seek professional help to see them through their struggles while working toward change. Fortunately, with the techniques shared in this book, you can take the initial steps. Get back to basics to get your life back on track. Remember that you're likely fighting against months or years of negative thinking, so you have to make an equally intense effort to fight through on your journey to achieve your desired results and maintain a consistent way of thinking. If you take this lightly and are not consistent with your efforts, you risk falling right back into your trap because of things like negativity bias at work in the background.

Now that you have a clear understanding of what negative thoughts are, how they come about, and ways to identify them, you can use the tools shared in the book to overcome them, including

- reshaping your mind.

- becoming your own best friend.

- using thought exercises to combat negative thinking.

- defeating negative thought patterns with communication.

- exercising compassion.
- exercising gratitude in its fullest form.
- journaling your thoughts.
- adopting habits that will allow you to embrace change.
- capitalizing on self-affirmation.
- empowering yourself through mindfulness and meditation.

Remember to make this journey personal by finding what works best for you and staying true to that path. Now you have what you need to take that first step into a better world while you work toward conquering fear, anxiety, stress, and depression. If you enjoyed this book and would like to recommend it to other readers who may be looking for answers to similar questions that you've had, please leave a review. Until then, have a great journey ahead. I'm confident you'll make it through!

References

Anxiety and negative thoughts. (n.d.). https://www.calmclinic.com/anxiety/symptoms/bad-thoughts

Break negative thinking with these 6 mental health exercises. (n.d.). CNET. https://www.cnet.com/health/mental/break-negative-thinking-with-these-6-mental-health-exercises/

Building self-esteem by changing negative thoughts. (n.d.). https://www.mentalhelp.net/self-esteem/changing-negative-thoughts/

Catastrophizing: what is it and how to stop. (2016, May 17). Psych Central. https://psychcentral.com/lib/what-is-catastrophizing#how-to-stop

Challenging negative thoughts: helpful tips. (2021, September 13). Psych Central. https://psychcentral.com/lib/challenging-negative-self-talk#self-talk-and-self-doubt

How gratitude attracts more things to be thankful for. (n.d.). LinkedIn https://www.linkedin.com/pulse/how-gratitude-attracts-more-things-thankful-tony-walker/

How to turn negative thoughts into positive thoughts. (2022, December 6). Mental Health Center Kids. https://mentalhealthcenterkids.com/blogs/articles/turning-negative-thoughts-into-positive

Jumping to conclusions: when people decide based on insufficient information (n.d.). Effectiviology. https://effectiviology.com/jumping-to-conclusions/

Mayo Clinic. (2017, October 13). *Generalized anxiety disorder* . Mayo Clinic. https://www.mayoclinic.org/diseases-conditions/generalized-anxiety-disorder/symptoms-causes/syc-20360803

News in Health. (2017, June 28). *Mindfulness matters.* NIH News in Health. https://newsinhealth.nih.gov/2012/01/mindfulness-matters#:~:text=Studies%20suggest%20that%20mindfulness%20practices

O'Brien, C. (2020, January 10). *21/90 Good habits and a great life.* Active Iron. https://www.activeiron.com/blog/the-21-90-rule-make-life-better/#:~:text=Build%20a%20habit%20and%20make

Outreach. (2021, November 19). *Negative thought patterns and depression.* Sage Neuroscience Center. https://sageclinic.org/blog/negative-thoughts-depression/

resource. (n.d.). Psychology Tools. https://www.psychologytools.com/resource/emotional-reasoning/

Ring, M. (2014, September 30). *Find a way to serve -.* Meaningring.com. https://meaningring.com/2014/10/01/find-a-way-to-serve-by-jack-canfield/#:~:text=The%20greatest%20levels%20of%20contentment

Smookler, E. (2023, June 2). *How to be your own best friend.* Mindful. https://www.mindful.org/how-to-be-your-own-best-friend/

Taylor, M. (n.d.). *What to know about positive affirmations.* WebMD. https://www.webmd.com/balance/what-to-know-positive-affirmations#:~:text=The%20purpose%20of%20positive%20affirmations

The difficulty with emotional reasoning (2023, September 23) Choice House. (n.d.). https://www.choicehousecolorado.com/the-difficulty-with-emotional-reasoning/#:~:text=Overcoming%20Emotional%20Reasoning&text=Therefore%2C%20mindfulness%2C%20journaling%2C%20and

The power of compassion Compassionate Communities NI. (n.d.). https://compassionatecommunitiesni.com/the-power-of-compassion/

The World Counts. (n.d.). https://www.theworldcounts.com/purpose/what-is-labeling-theory-psychology

Triggers: what they are, how they form, and what to do. (2022, April 28). Psych Central. https://psychcentral.com/lib/what-is-a-trigger#examples

Understanding negative thoughts feelings | On my mind | Anna Freud Centre. (n.d.). https://www.annafreud.org/on-my-mind/self-care/understanding-negative-thoughts-and-feelings/#:~:text=Understanding%20negative%20thoughts%20and%20feelings&text=It

University of Rochester Medical Center. (2022). *Journaling for mental health - health encyclopedia -* University of Rochester Medical Center. https://www.urmc.rochester.edu/encyclopedia/content.aspx?ContentID=4552&ContentTypeID=1#:~:text=Journaling%20helps%20control%20your%20symptoms

What causes negative thinking and how to stop it. (n.d.). Baptist Health. https://www.baptisthealth.com/blog/family-health/what-causes-negative-thinking-and-how-to-stop-it

What is catastrophizing? 6 ways to stop catastrophic thinking. (2018, February 7). https://www.medicalnewstoday.com/articles/320844#related-conditions

What is overgeneralization? (n.d.). Verywell Mind. https://www.verywellmind.com/overgeneralization-3024614#:~:text=Research%20has%20also%20found%20that

What Is Overgeneralizing? | Psychology Today South Africa. (n.d.). https://www.psychologytoday.com/za/blog/all-the-rage/201908/what-is-overgeneralizing

Change your thinking (2023). Mindforlife.org. https://www.mindforlife.org/change-your-thinking/

Printed in Dunstable, United Kingdom